<u>Testimonials</u>

In all of politics, there is only one question and that is, "who decides"? Should the nexus of decision making be the coercive power of the state or individuals making decisions for themselves? Only individuals working with their doctors, can hold all of the information about their unique situation. This decision making should not be abdicated to a nameless faceless bureaucracy that cannot know what is best for everyone. I worked as doctor in Canada or many years and the people there have chosen the nameless faceless bureaucracy over individual autonomy. The result is a system rife with dysfunction and a paucity of quality care. When I was Medical Director for Diagnostic Imaging in Thunder Bay, Canada, our wait time for a CT scan was seven months and for an MRI scan, it was 13 months. Many in the US desire that we go down the path of more government control of health care. Dr. Sabrin proposes a better way. One based on individual decision making empowering the sacrosanct doctor-patient relationship for the best possible care and with rational pricing predicated on competition and choice. It is time that we heed Dr. Sabrin's advice.

Lee Kurisko MD
Author; Health Reform - The End of the American Revolution?

Economics is our most beneficial science. Its practitioners seek to demonstrate how to increase well being for all participants in markets. They've delivered their promise in many of those markets, but the American medical care market is not one of them.

Economist Murray Sabrin demonstrates why. Another term for free-dom of choice in markets is personal responsibility. Throughout life, we accept and embrace individual accountability as we pursue better-ment for ourselves and others. Except in medical care, where we have forfeited responsibility to an array of special interests who want us to be sick. Foremost among those are governments, for whom sickness means dependency, on which they thrive. Pharmaceutical companies and insurance companies embrace sickness-as-a-business. Big food, big alcohol, and big tobacco don't help.

Sabrin identifies two routes out of this dead end. First, personal responsibility for the pursuit of well being. Good personal practice based on readily available information about diet, nutrition, exer-cise and good habits could eliminate up to 80% of chronic ill-health conditions of the US population. Second, personal responsibility for payment and use of medical services, based on the individual as sin-gle-payer, health savings accounts, catastrophic insurance, plus the charitable and community services that emerge in healthy popula-tions, would replace the convoluted unaffordable government-de-signed regulatory, payment and delivery bureaucracy.

This book is deeply researched, incisively informative, logically sound, and highly persuasive about the right future for medical care in America. Since the current state is demonstrably unsustainable, Sabrin's book is vita

Hunter Hastings
Economics For Business
Mises Institute
Lee Kurisko MD
Author; Health Reform - The End of the American Revolution?

Dr. Sabrin's book provides solid alternative solutions to the quagmire that has become the American medical system. The present system is too costly, too bureaucratic, and too authoritarian. Patients are often not able to choose their doctor, and are forced to pay for services they do not want and cannot use. Sabrin advocates returning power to the people who actually receive the medical services. Adoption of his suggestions would go a long way toward making the medical system more affordable and responsive to the needs of the people who use medical services, which is all of us.

Robert W. McGee, JD, PhD, DSc, CPA (ret.)
Fayetteville State University

Universal Medical Care from Conception to End of Life is the perfect prescription for you, if you want to understand why our medical insurance and provider industries are terminally sick. Dr. M. Sabrin (PhD.) beautifully writes on these pages the complete understanding of why it happened and where it is headed. But more importantly, he gives you the medicine to have hope, self-protect, save money and have better medical care.

Dwight Carey, serial startup entrepreneur
involved with over 200 startup ventures.
Professor of Entrepreneurship
Business and Engineering
Temple University

Universal Medical Care from Conception to End of Life

The Case for a Single-Payer System

Murray Sabrin, PH.D.

PAGE PUBLISHING, INC.
Conneaut Lake, PA

First originally published by Page Publishing 2021

ISBN 978-1-6624-3336-8 (pbk)
ISBN 978-1-6624-3337-5 (digital)

Printed in the United States of America

Contents

Introduction

Why has medical care become so complicated—and expensive? Not very long ago, an individual would visit a doctor to be treated for an illness that could not be "cured" by one of Grandma's "recipes." Whether it was a sore throat, earache, or digestive pain, Grandma usually had some homespun "medicine" to deal with a common medical issue. And if Grandma's "medicine chest" was not able to deal with a family member's illness, a neighborhood doctor was usually available to treat working families at his office, or he would make a house call for a reasonable fee.

Baby boomers who grew up in the 1950s, especially in a big city, would be taken by their parents to a doctor's office and would pay a modest fee somewhere in the range of five dollars per visit. There would be no insurance forms and therefore no co-pays, no deductibles for a routine office visit. If a prescription drug was required, families paid out of pocket for relatively inexpensive antibiotics and other necessary medications. If a medical test was needed, families usually paid for it out of pocket. But if an operation was required, working families usually had a major medical policy through their employer that covered virtually all the expenses—anesthesiology, surgery, and, of course, hospitalization.

Overtime, with the passage of Medicare and Medicaid in July 1965 and the acceleration of price inflation beginning in the Johnson administration who gave us the notorious "guns and butter" policies to fight simultaneously the Vietnam War and the war on poverty better known as the Great Society, both private and public medical insurance began to cover more and more routine expenses that historically had been paid for out of pocket.

Instead of medical insurance covering only catastrophic incidences, such as heart operations, cancer treatments, and other major medical procedures, the American people have come to expect that medical insurance would pay for virtually all their expenses after they met a deductible and paid a small co-pay. In effect, medical insurance has been turned on its head by essentially creating "prepayment plans" through their employer who has become the first medical "gatekeeper" for employees and their families. So instead of families being in charge of what medical coverage they want, employers basically offer cookie-cutter policies to their employees, putting insurance companies in charge of what can and cannot be covered in network, out of network, etc.

Is the current system of providing medical care, namely, through employer-based insurance, Medicare, and Medicaid, the optimal methods to provide high-quality, low-cost care to all Americans?

The answer is a resounding no. *Universal Medical Care from Conception to End of Life: The Case for a Single-Payer System* explains why the current system of both private employer-based insurance and government programs, such as Medicare, Medicaid, and Obamacare, is financially untenable and yields less than optimal outcomes for patients. Yet there are calls for more top-down approaches to medical care, most notably by Senator Bernie Sanders, who has campaigned for the presidency on a Medicare for All program, essentially putting all Americans under one medical umbrella, where the government would set all the parameters for medical care.

In other words, the Medicare for All proposal gives more power to the government not only over the American people but also over doctors, hospitals, pharmaceutical companies, and other medical providers. Medicare for All puts patients at the mercy of government bureaucrats "to do the right thing" regarding the medical care for 330 million Americans.

But there is a better way, a proven way to give individuals what they want at reasonable prices. As economist, historian, and libertarian philosopher Murray Rothbard pointed out, "The picture of the free market is necessarily one of harmony and mutual benefit; the picture of State intervention is one of caste conflict, coercion, and exploitation."

Under a single-payer system outlined here, with every American adult in charge of their medical coverage, there would be no more conflicts regarding insurance companies paying for abortion, contraception, and other controversial medical procedure and medications. In other words, in a free market, an individual pays for what he/she wants.

And as Tennessee Congressman Jim Cooper observed, "Almost every economist agrees that the American health care system is unsustainable. Medical care is so expensive that it is busting all of our budgets—government, business, and personal. Eventually, the medical price bubble will pop. What, then, are the alternatives?"

The short answer—the free market where the doctor-patient relationship is restored, people take personal responsibility for their health care, and medical insurance is only needed for catastrophic illnesses.

As Dr. Eugene Cheslock, founder of the Parker Family Health Center (Red Bank, New Jersey) pointed out regarding personal responsibility and other medical issues.

> I guess it is too much to ask that a person safeguard his/her precious gift of life by adopting good habits and avoiding the excesses, and indulgences, too many to elaborate. Why is the good caretaker responsible for the abused?
>
> The other factor never addressed is the impact of defensive medicine on the cost of care. Frivolous litigation, much more common here than in so many other industrialized nations, adds billions to the medical costs and leads to the premature retirement of healthcare professionals and probably deters them from pursuing careers in medicine in the first place.

> The expectations of the American public are also exaggerated leading to even more challenges for the system.
>
> What the public and the legislators and the lawyers fail to appreciate is how special and unique each individual is, how unpredictable outcomes may be, how reactions to therapeutics are totally unknown, first time around. And, the recourse in these situations is the courts.

The following chapters will challenge the American people to rethink their general support for the medical care status quo in the United States. Furthermore, under my proposal, social harmony will increase because individuals, not employers, insurance companies, nor the government, will make medical decisions that should be left to patients and their doctors.

Chapter 1, "The Rise of the Welfare State in America," will explain the roots of America's welfare state and how the Great Depression cemented dependency on the federal government for basic necessities, which eventually led to massive government intervention in medicine.

Chapter 2, "Restoring the Doctor-Patient Relationship with Free Markets and Essential Insurance," examines the pros and cons of a free market in medicine. The chapter will explain how households can regain control of medical decisions without the need for third-party payers except for catastrophic insurance.

Chapter 3, "Medicare, Medicaid, and Obamacare and the Path to an Individual Single-Payer System," will outline the strengths and weaknesses of government involvement in medical care. The framework for transitioning to a free market medical care system will be outlined.

Chapter 4, "Nonprofits and Voluntarism: Society's Effective Safety Net," explains how the nonprofit sector will become an integral component of a free market solution to Medicaid.

Chapter 5, "Wellness, Optimal Health, and Personal Responsibility," reviews why adults need to be informed about how to obtain optimal health in order to avoid costly medical bills. A healthy population will have an enormous impact on reducing the nation's medical costs, thereby saving hundreds of billions of dollars that then could be used for other outlays that would increase living standards.

Chapter 6, "Pandemic, Lockdowns, and the Doctor-Patient Relationship," coronavirus, medical care, and government failure will review the different responses of federal and state governments to the pandemic of 2020. There is a growing body of evidence that the "top-down" approach to deal with the pandemic has been counterproductive and how free markets would have dealt with the pandemic.

Chapter 7, "Toward the Individual Single-Payer Medical Care System," is a summary of how free market medical care—the individual single-payer system—would empower individuals and families and provide them with high-quality health care at affordable prices.

I would like to thank the following individuals for their comments and suggestions, Dr. Eugene Cheslock, Angela Daidone, Suzanne Dwyer, Andrea Egan, Amanda Missey, Joseph Sansone, and of course, my wife, Florence M. Sabrin, who improved the manuscript with her keen edits.

In addition, I would like to thank several physicians and other medical experts whom I interviewed for their insights about the medical system: Dr. Rebekah Bernard, Dr. David Cunningham, Dr. Alieta Eck, Dr. Glenn Gero, Dr. Lee Kurisco, Dr. Keith Smith, and Ralph Weber.

And a special thanks to my research assistants, Cody Collins, Will Sperduto, and Eric Soger. I would also thank The Charles Koch Institute for providing me with a grant to work on this research project in the spring 2017. The ideas and views expressed in the book are my responsibility. Lastly, I would like to thank Page Publishing for shaping the manuscript into his final form.

Chapter 1

The Rise of the Welfare State in America

The Welfare State is merely a method for transforming
the market economy step by step into socialism.
—Ludwig von Mises

Government, by its nature, is not compassionate. It can't be. It is
nothing other than a force. Government can only spend a dollar to
help someone when it forcibly takes a dollar from someone else…
At its core, government welfare is predicated on false compassion.
—Stephen Moore

From each according to his ability to each according to his needs.
—Karl Marx

To begin a heated argument even among the best of friends,
mention the welfare system. Liberals generally support and
want to expand the government's role—at all levels—to
assist people who are not financially independent. Conservatives
assert they oppose the welfare state and want to cut back on benefits by introducing "tough love" so people can get back on their feet
instead of being a burden on their fellow citizens.

Nevertheless, an extensive welfare system has been a permanent
fixture of American society since the Great Depression, when the federal government took on the responsibility of supporting individuals

and families with cash payments and other benefits as the employment rate was peaking at 25 percent in 1933. But even as the economy improved ever so slowly, despite the enormous sums on what now is broadly described as social welfare spending by the federal government, additional federal programs were enacted under both Republican and Democratic administrations during the past eighty years to provide benefits for poor families as well as middle-income households. Thus, despite their anti-welfare rhetoric Republicans have raised the white flag in their "opposition" to the welfare state, which means in effect they have become "junior partners" in the cementing—and expanding—President Johnson's Great Society and FDR's New Deal.

Before we explore how and why Republicans have embraced the welfare state, let's ask, Why does America have a welfare state in the first place? After all, colonists and Americans in the early days of the Republic were generally considered a hardy bunch of "rugged individualists," who created voluntary associations to address the risks of life in the vast continent they began to inhabit as they arrived from Europe and other regions of the world. America's melting pot, in other words, eschewed welfarism because it was not part of their core social values.

Another aspect of America's welfare state, namely, corporate welfare, which is an egregious example of redistributing money from low- and middle-income families to the politically connected and financial elites of America, has given free markets and capitalism a black eye. So while social welfare spending has skyrocketed for decades, both Republicans and Democrats have supported corporate welfare because they have asserted it creates jobs and improves American business competitiveness around the world. The evidence tells a different story, however. Corporate welfare spending distorts the economy and enriches businesses, which claim to be free enterprise supporters but nonetheless have no qualms lobbying for government grants, subsidies, and contracts paid with taxpayer dollars. A vast amount of literature critical of corporate welfare is available at Mises.org, Fee.org, Aier.org, Fff.org, Cato.org, and other free market organizations.

America's welfare state did not begin with the birth of the Republic when the Constitution was ratified on September 17, 1787, at the convention of the states in Philadelphia. The idea of an American welfare state germinated in the late nineteenth century and bloomed throughout the twentieth century with the creation of Social Security (1935), the addition of the Cabinet Department Health, Education, and Welfare (HEW, 1953), Medicare and Medicaid (1965), and into the twenty-first century with the expansion of Medicare under President George W. Bush and the passage of President Obama's signature piece of legislation, the Affordable Care Act, popularly known as Obamacare.

The growth in welfare spending, which is comprised of approximately eighty means tested program—from Medicaid, the State Children's Health Insurance Program (SCHIP), the Supplemental Nutrition Assistance Program (SNAP [formerly known as food stamps]), Women, Infants, and Children (WIC), Section 8 housing vouchers, Temporary Assistance to Needy Families (TANF), Pell Grants, farm subsidies, Head Start, Supplemental Security Income (SSI), school breakfast and lunch programs, and Low Income Home Energy Assistance Program (LIHEAP), among others—will so overwhelm the federal budget that major cuts in these programs and/or tax increases will have to occur to keep the federal government's books in balance.

As well intentioned as welfare programs are, they are counterproductive—for both welfare recipients and taxpayers.

Welfare programs create a culture of dependency and thus prevent individuals and families from becoming financially independent. In addition, taxpayers are forced to support welfare programs that reduce their living standards today and make it harder for them to save for their future. Also, taxpayers have less money to make charitable contributions in their own communities.

Instead of "trickle-down welfarism"—which has been entrenched in America for more than eight decades—taxpayers should receive a one-dollar federal tax credit for every dollar they donate to a recognized IRS charity. This tax change would make the most effective social service charities—as well as colleges, universities, and hospitals—in the country financially stronger so they can provide more needed services in their communities. We would then be able to phase out welfare programs and create a "culture of caring" that would give the least fortunate in our communities a helping hand instead of taxpayers being forced to support their neighbors, many of whom spend years or decades in financial dependency.

As we shall see in this chapter, although Democrats gave birth to the welfare state, the current GOP, the party of self-styled fiscal conservatives and limited government, has supported the growth of the welfare state even when they controlled the White House and one or more houses of Congress. Rhetorically, Republicans have "opposed" the welfare state and on numerous occasions expressed concern about the growth of entitlement spending, but, with very few exceptions, have they questioned the legitimacy of federal welfare programs and spending? Thus, fiscal conservatism died a long time ago in Washington DC without a proper funeral, and very few in Congress have mourned the demise of limiting—let alone reducing—federal government social welfare spending.

The federal budget has been increasing continuously no matter who occupies the White House or controls Congress. Accordingly, America's "two-party system" is effectively a myth when it comes to the big picture—government spending. There is only one party in DC, the Washington Party, with two wings: big spending Democrats and big spending Republicans.

This chapter will explore the philosophical foundations of the welfare state, the evolution of America's welfare state, the pros and cons of the welfare state, and why the cornerstone of the welfare state's medical programs—Medicare and Medicaid and now Obamacare—must be replaced with a sustainable approach to medical care based upon free markets and nonprofitization—and personal responsibility. Moreover, the private medical insurance market has been grossly distorted by federal regulations and by a massive amount of cronyism—obtaining special government privileges receiving taxpayer dollars and restricting competition. Restructuring American medicine will not be an easy task, but the road map in the following chapters will pave the way for a less costly and higher-quality medical "system" that will be based upon "we the people" using fundamental free market principles and sound financial practices. In addition, medical care must be based on the doctor-patient relationship so patients come first instead of insurance and pharmaceutical companies and welfare state advocates in the federal government, academia, and the media.

America's Philosophical Roots

The preamble to the United States Constitution lays down the objectives of the fledgling Republic that was created nearly 240 years ago, which public officials and naturalized citizens should all be familiar with when they take an oath to support the Constitution. Moreover, every youngster and college student should have learned about the Constitution in an American history or social studies class. Nevertheless, there seems to be substantial ambiguity in the minds of many Americans about the meaning of the preamble—and the Constitution in general. So what exactly does the preamble state?

> We the people of the United States, in order to form a more perfect union, establish justice, ensure domestic tranquility, *provide for the common defense, promote the general welfare* and secure the blessings of liberty to ourselves and our posterity, do ordain and establish this Constitution for the United States of America. (Emphasis added)

What did the founders mean when they wrote that the federal government would "promote the general welfare?" Did the founders believe that the federal government would "provide" what we generally consider federal welfare spending today—income payments, food stamps, retirement benefits, medical insurance, housing subsidies, and other federal expenditures?

The preamble, however, does call for the Constitution to "provide for the common defense." Clearly, the founders understood the difference between "provide" and "promote," which is clarified in Article I, Section 8. In Article I, Section 8 the writers of the Constitution did not include any authorized activity of the federal government that in any way can be construed as social welfare spending. Section 8 does outline unequivocally the duties of the federal government, such as borrowing money, coining money, establishing post offices supporting an army in the Navy, declaring war, and other very narrow duties in order to establish a free Republic so that the people would "secure the blessings of liberty."

Article I, Section 8 also states, "Congress shall…provide for the common defense and general welfare of the United States." When something is provided, it generally means it is given, made available, such as parents providing their children with a college education; in other words, the parents *would pay* for their children's education. In Section 8, when the founders wrote "provide for the general welfare," they did not include social welfare spending in any of the specific duties of the federal government. In short, if the founders wanted to create a comprehensive welfare state, they would've stated the specific welfare spending that the Congress would be authorized to undertake. They did not. Instead, the Tenth Amendment states unambiguously, "The powers not delegated to the United States by the Constitution, nor prohibited by it to the states, are reserved to the states respectively, or to the people." Thus, a logical conclusion of the founders' intent regarding the responsibilities of the federal government would be that the *states or the people* would deliver any social welfare spending, not the new federal government.

Virtually, all members of Congress would disagree with the above analysis, except maybe a few who took their *oath* seriously that they would uphold the Constitution. What we have seen above is that the Constitution does not authorize the federal government to "provide" specific social welfare spending. And most of the talking heads in the media and professors in numerous disciplines would strenuously object that the Constitution should be interpreted in such a narrow way. But the Constitution speaks for itself—no social welfare spending is authorized. In other words, the original intent of the founders has been clear for more than two hundred years, but the federal courts, especially the Supreme Court, have upheld the incremental shift of the country from a limited government Republic to a comprehensive welfare state.

In a previous era, such as the one that gave us the Eighteenth Amendment prohibiting the manufacture and sale of alcohol, lawmakers realized that if it's not in the Constitution, the founding document has to be amended. Faithfulness to the Constitution has been replaced by removing the chains Thomas Jefferson said would bind legislators from creating mischief. And then there's George Mason who pointed out (1776) in the Virginia Declaration of Rights, "No free government, or the blessings of liberty, can be preserved to any people but by a firm adherence to justice, moderation, temperance, frugality, and virtue."

The Creation and Growth of the Welfare State

America's welfare state has had three distinct stages. Economist William Anderson described them in his essay ("The Genesis of Welfare," *The Free Market,* July 1998, mises.org/library/genesis-welfare) as follows:

> The first significant push for welfare came during the beginning of the Progressive Era the late 1800s, a time when average economic growth was the highest it has ever been in US history. The second great pushed occurred during the 1930s after the recovery from the worst of the Great Depression had already begun. The third, and possibly the most harmful, phase came in 1960s during the long economic expansion when President. Lyndon Johnson convinced Congress to implement his "Great Society" programs.

According to Anderson, the intellectual and moral justification for a welfare state rest upon a dubious assertion. But that assertion has gained traction for more than a hundred years because "politicians, program administrators, and recipients of largess [were able] to convince the taxpaying public that the welfare state is a social necessity which 'humanizes' capitalism and provides a 'safety net' for the most vulnerable individuals." Ironically, America's welfare state was created when the US economy was booming in the late nineteenth century, which was punctuated at times with an occasional banking panic, and grew markedly when the US economy was booming in the 1960s. The thesis, therefore, that "hard" economic times sparked the demand for government social welfare programs is flawed given the historical evidence. However, the Great Depression was the catalyst for changing the public's perception that a welfare state was in the best interests of the American people. The conventional thinking as the Depression unfolded—and ever since—is that capitalism is "unstable" and so "risky" that a federal government safety net it is essential for the general welfare of the American people.

As we shall see, whatever short-term benefits the welfare state has provided the American people, which ignores the opportunity costs that individuals, families, and business owners have had to incur, a fact that is basically ignored by the proponents of welfarism, the long-term negative consequences are real and have arrived and have been unfolding for decades as politicians of both major parties have undertaken an orgy of spending to provide the American people from the cradle to the grave. In addition, public opinion molders, including most of my fellow academics, have been beating the drums for the welfare state for more than a century.

Nevertheless, even today, there are conservatives and libertarians who argue that the welfare state is here to stay and that opposition to the welfare state is futile. Obviously, these so-called free market advocates do not subscribe to Winston Churchill's passionate plea during World War II to his British countrymen, "We will never surrender." Apparently, surrendering to the ideology of the welfare state is the path of least resistance for "inside the beltway" pundits and think tank writers who want to be "respectable" and remain relevant and uncontroversial in the great battle of ideas, welfarism versus liberty. This is a losing strategy. A strategy to abolish the welfare state's medical care intervention and replace it with an enduring, sustainable, and compassionate approach to health care and social services is imperative for the country. We must work tirelessly to regain the lost freedoms that the welfare state has diminished over the past several decades. The following chapters will outline not only the strategy to pursue but also the practical alternatives to third-party insurance, Medicare, Medicaid, and Obamacare.

Religion, Self-Interest Ideology, and the Rise of the Welfare State

What are the ideological underpinnings of the welfare state that the welfare bureaucracies have embraced? What is the origin of America's welfare state? There are several theories that have been developed to explain how America became a welfare state. One theory asserts that industrialization and urbanization of nineteenth century caused the masses to demand the welfare state to provide them with security given the uncertainty of the market economy and "alienation" of urban living. This seemingly plausible explanation that the drive to create a welfare state was in effect a mass movement generated by the "poor, the masses, or the oppressed working-class" falls apart when the evidence is examined.

Upon closer examination, the United States industrialized more rapidly than European countries, which adopted social welfare policies sooner than America. In other words, researchers found "no correlation between levels of industrialization and socialization insurance programs of 12 European nations between the 1880s and the 1920s."

Were labor unions instrumental in creating the welfare state so the members would be "protected" from the vicissitudes of the free market? This assertion does not hold up to scrutiny because of the relatively negligible impact of labor unions on the US economy. Unions, however, did have major impacts and flourished in the coal industry and the building trades before welfare state policies were enacted.

In an extensive essay published ("Origins of the Welfare State in America," *Journal of Libertarian Studies*, Fall 1996) shortly after his death in 1995 economist, historian, and political philosopher Murray Rothbard addressed these assertions and reached the following conclusion. America's welfare state was created because of the confluence the following factors. Rothbard pointed out that ideology, including religious beliefs and economic interest, were "two forces that joined together to bring about the welfare state."

Rothbard made the following observations. First, religious ideas promulgated by many Protestant churches in the northeast region of the country beginning around 1830 focused on "each believers' sacred duty to devote his energies to trying to establish a Kingdom of God on Earth, to establishing the perfect society in America and eventually the world, to stamp out sin, to 'make America holy'..." Against this backdrop, Rothbard pointed out that the agenda of the so-called Yankees was clear: government was needed for the salvation of individuals, the following goals proclaimed, prohibition, abolition of slavery, and making Sunday a day of rest. Not only religious leaders considered ending slavery a moral imperative but a growing consensus all Americans viewed slavery as an abhorrent institution. Second, two economic special interest groups supported America's welfare state experiment. "One was a growing legion of educated [and often overeducated] intellectuals, technocrats, and the 'helping professions' who sought power, prestige, subsidies, contracts, cushy jobs from the welfare state, and restrictions of entry into the field forms licensing. The second was groups of big businessmen who, after failing to achieve monopoly power on the free market, turned to government—local, state, and federal—to gain it for them. The government would provide subsidies, contracts and, particularly, an enforced collateralization. After 1900, these two groups coalesced, combining two crucial elements: wealth individuals and opinion-molding power, the latter no longer hampered by the resistance of the Democratic Party committed to laissez-faire ideology. The new coalition joined together to create and accelerate the welfare state in America."

Another element in the creation of a comprehensive welfare state in America was the establishment of the Women's Christian Temperance Union (WCTU) in 1874. In addition to calling for the prohibition of alcohol, the WCTU was instrumental in supporting widespread government intervention to improve social welfare. "These measures included the outlawing of license brothels and red light districts, imposition of maximum eight hour working day, the establishment of government facilities for neglected and dependent children, government shelters for children of working mothers, government recreation facilities for the urban poor, federal aid to education, mother's education by government, and government vocational training for women." Also, the WCTU reported lowering the age for kindergarten so educational professionals could guide children early in life.

Perhaps one of the most influential proponents of establishing welfare state in America was the economist Richard T. Ely, founder of the American Economic Association, who graduated from Columbia University in 1876. Ely wanted to obtain a PhD. He studied in Germany with other Americans who wanted to study history, philosophy, and other social sciences. (The United States did not offer this terminal degree as of 1880s.) At age twenty-eight, Ely became an instructor in political economy at Johns Hopkins University, America's first graduate university. After being denied a full professorship at Hopkins, Ely became a professor at the University of Wisconsin in 1892 and director of the Institute, the School of Economics, Political Science, and History. In addition to his academic work, Ely became an adviser to Progressive Governor Robert M. LaFollette, who adopted many social welfare programs at the state level.

To understand the passion of Ely and other nineteenth century welfare state opponents, the following statement by him sums up the ideology that is the underlying foundation for their embrace of the welfare state, "God works through the State in carrying out His purpose more universally and to any other institution." And this grandiose purpose is to create a "New Jerusalem" in America.

As Ely and others were creating the theoretical framework for the welfare state, "Yankee women Progressives provided the shock troops the progressive movement and hence the burning welfare state." Jane Addams, one of the leading proponents of the welfare state, devoted her life to working in Chicago slums. Addams's colleague at Hull House Julia Clifford Lathrop was an important figure in the spread of social welfare ideas in America. In 1912, President William Howard Taft appointed her head of the first US Children's Bureau. "After World War I, and the Children's Bureau lobbied for, and pushed through Congress in late 1921 the Shepherd-Towner Paternity and Infancy Protection Act, providing federal funds to states that set up child hygiene for child welfare bureaus, as well as providing public instruction in maternal and infant care by nurses and physicians. Here we had the beginnings of socialized medicine as well as the socialized family."

The next generation social welfare proponents, most of whom born in the 1880s, a generation after Richard Ely and his cohort began agitating for government—that is, taxpayer financed—social programs, included such notable figures as future First Lady Eleanor Roosevelt, future Secretary of Labor Frances Perkins, and FDR's close confidant Harry Lloyd Hopkins.

As the next generation of welfare proponents was being born in the 1880s, in Germany, Chancellor Otto von Bismarck was sponsoring a comprehensive welfare state in response to the popularity of the social Democrats. As Richard Ebeling recounts ("Marching to Bismarck's Drummer: The Origins of the Modern Welfare State," https://fee.org/articles/marching-to-bismarcks-drummer-the-origins-of-the-modern-welfare-state/), Bismarck supported legislation that "guaranteed every German national health insurance, of pension, a minimum wage and workplace regulation, vacation and unemployment insurance." Bismarck explained his support for these left-wing proposals by stating, "My idea was to bribe the working classes, or shall I say, to win them over, to regard the state as a social institution existing for their sake and interested in their welfare." Moreover, the welfare state "ideology" was rooted in the belief that welfarism was the logical evolution of human development. As one American admirer of the German welfare state observed, "the individual exists for the state, not the state for the individual."

With the election of Franklin Delano Roosevelt in 1932, America's welfare state took a great leap forward with his New Deal programs. This episode in American history illustrates Robert Higgs's thesis that a "crisis," in this case the onset of the Great Depression, made it possible for FDR to propose and expand the role of government in America, especially by providing direct monetary benefits to the unemployed and others suffering during the greatest economic downturn in our history.

Of all FDR's social welfare programs, Social Security has become the so-called third rail of American politics because if a politician tries to tamper, tinker with it, the voters "zap" him at the polling booth. Because of the popularity of Social Security, the accepted narrative is that FDR proposed Social Security to provide old-age security for working folks in America, and businesses opposed it lock, stock, and barrel. The evidence suggests otherwise. According to Rothbard, "[Big business] almost all back the Social Security scheme to the hilt while it was attacked by such associations of small business as the National Metal Trades Association, the Illinois Manufacturing Association, and the National Association of Manufacturers. By 1939, only 17% of American businesses favored repeal of the Social Security Act, while not one big business firm supported repeal."

A common view of business is that they all have the same interests, namely, little or no government intervention in the marketplace. The creation of Social Security shows that many big business interests wanted to raise the cost of doing business for smaller enterprises and thus make them less competitive in the marketplace.

The historical record could not be any clearer; ideology buttressed by religious doctrines laid the welfare state foundation that grew over the past hundred years. And when a crisis occurred, the opportunistic political class had little opposition in expanding the welfare state in America. Not surprisingly then, there has emerged a bipartisan consensus in Washington DC to maintain the so-called social safety net for the country's most vulnerable citizens. The "debate" in Washington DC revolves around a single issue: how much should the welfare state grow a year, not whether we should have a welfare state.

Postwar Boom and the Great Society

When President Johnson outlined his Great Society vision on May 22, 1964, at a University of Michigan commencement address, he saw an America where there was still much poverty amid abundance, undereducated youngsters and adults because of failing schools. He proposed a joint venture between the federal government and local authorities in what he called "a creative federalism" to tackle "the crushing weight of poverty." LBJ also decried the racial injustice that held back America's minority citizens.

But as William Anderson pointed out in his welfare essay, "Poverty rates were plummeting in the United States, and especially for blacks, from more than thirty-three percent in the early 1950s to less than fifteen percent by the late 1960s. In other words, 'dog-eat-dog' capitalism and the philanthropic sector it created were helping to eradicate poverty on its own." Despite the best of intentions and massive amounts of federal government expenditures, the poverty rate in America essentially flatlined after the introduction of the Great Society in the mid to late 1960s.

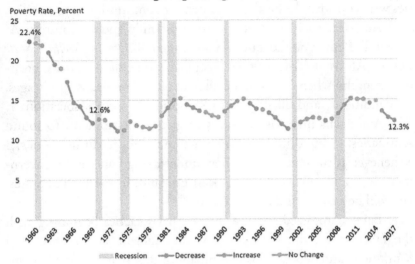

Figure 1

Anderson also observed, "Although it was clear nearly from the start that the 'Great Society' was a colossal failure, groups of well-dressed and well-educated suburbanites agitated for its expansion. While the stated reasons were 'compassion for the poor,' it turned out that the greatest recipients of this new largess were middle-class government employees." Moreover, according to Anderson, "New York City's financial crisis of the mid-1970s came precisely because city officials had managed to turn Gotham into one great welfare state, including tuition-free education from preschool through graduate school, free hospitalization, and hundreds of other 'benefits,' which were financed mostly by overtaxed businesses."

The Rise of Voluntary Associations

Although there were elements of the welfare state in colonial America (Jonathan R. T. Hughes, *The Governmental Habit* 1977), the idea of national welfare state was anathema to most Americans.

In fact, in the early days of the Republic, the so-called helping activities were considered a local government or community responsibility.

America's social culture focused on family and community. As David T. Beito pointed out (*From Mutual Aid to the Welfare State* 2000), Alexis de Tocqueville recognized one of America's greatest strengths when he (Tocqueville) wrote, "Americans of all ages, all conditions, and all dispositions constantly form associations... The Americans make associations to give entertainment, to found seminaries, to build inns, to construct churches, to diffuse books... Whenever at the end of some new undertaking you see the government in France, or a man of rank in England, in the United States, you will be sure to find an association."

Beito chronicled the rise of fraternal societies beginning with the Freemasons, the Odd Fellows, the Ancient Order of United Workmen, and scores of other organizations that attracted members throughout the country who received benefits, such as sick and disability payments, as well as life insurance for the beneficiaries. "Members of nearly all ethnic and national groups erected formidable networks of individual and collective self-help for protection."

The glue that held these organizations together was a value system based upon self-reliance, thrift, self-government, self-control, and good moral character. "These values reflected a fraternal consensus that cut across such seemingly intractable divisions as race, gender, income."

With the passage of the Social Security Act of 1935, the long decline of fraternal organizations began. Ironically, many fraternal leaders supported the expanding welfare state as a "logical extension of fraternalism" and a way to cut costs during the Great Depression. Nevertheless, some fraternal leaders expressed harsh criticism of the expanding welfare state. One fraternal leader stated, "Rugged individualism is crowded out and people lose their ambition and become listless as they dropped toward the valley of delusions called socialism."

In concluding his comprehensive study of fraternal societies, David Beito writes,

> The shift from mutual aid and self-help to the welfare state has involved more than a simple bookkeeping transfer of service provision from one set of institutions to another. As many of the leaders of fraternal societies have feared, much was lost in exchange that transcended monetary calculations. The old relationships of voluntary reciprocity and autonomy have slowly given way to paternalistic dependency. Instead of mutual aid, the dominant social welfare arrangements of Americans have increasingly become character-ized by impersonal bureaucracies controlled by outsiders.

Peter Drucker's Insights About the Welfare State

Very few observers and analysts of American business would quibble that Peter F. Drucker was the twentieth century's greatest management theoretician and business consultant. In his books, essays, articles, and consulting practice, spanning more than seven decades, Drucker's students and his clients have acknowledged his keen insights about successfully managing a business or nonprofit organization (https://vimeo.com/5068508).

For more than half a century, Drucker shaped the way we looked at business management, providing managers with the tools to make their enterprises more successful than they had been. And in the last two decades of his life, Drucker applied his insights about organizational behavior and structure as a consultant to nonprofit organizations. Therefore, it was not surprising that his essay, "It Profits Us to Strengthen Nonprofits," appeared on the editorial page of the *Wall Street Journal* (December 19, 1991), where he applied his half century of experience in calling for a new paradigm in dealing with social issues.

Given that the fiscal realities of the early 1990s, Drucker observes, "Federal, state and local governments will have to retrench sharply, no matter who is in office. *Moreover government has proved incompetent solving social problems. Virtually every success we have scored has been achieved by nonprofits*" (emphasis added). In addition, Drucker's other key points are the following: "many of the most heartening successes are being scored by small, local organizations"; "the average nonprofit must manage itself as well as the best managed ones do"; "nonprofits have to learn how to raise money"; "we need a change in the attitude of government and government bureaucracies." In the concluding section of his essay, Drucker asserts that government bureaucrats are in general hostile to nonprofits because "the success of the nonprofits undermines the bureaucracy's power and denies its *ideology*" (emphasis added). Drucker concluded that what is needed in America is quite simple: "a public policy that establishes the nonprofits as the country's first line of attack on social problems."

Drucker's essay provides fuel for critics of America's welfare state who see all levels of government engaging in counterproductive efforts to help lift people out of poverty and address some of the most intractable issues facing individuals and families, such as drug addiction, homelessness, and other social ills. But as Drucker pointed out, the entrenched bureaucracies' hostility toward nonprofits and ideological position are strong headwinds for his vision of "nonprofitization" to deal with social issues.

The Case for the Welfare State

Support for the welfare state comes from the usual suspects—liberals, progressives, democratic socialists, academics and, of course, politicians who are "true believers" and/ or see the welfare state as a means for boosting their election chances and reelection after they have convinced their constituents that "they are from the government and are here to help you." One academic, Teresa Ghilarducci, writing in *The Atlantic*, "The Welfare State: A Terrible Name for an Essential System," (December 3, 2015), begins her essay bemoaning the rise of the gig economy because workers are "shortchanged" inasmuch they typically do not receive employee benefits such as health insurance and do not receive unemployment benefits. In addition, gig workers typically do not have pensions and primarily have to rely on Social Security for the retirement income. Ghilarducci makes the Keynesian argument that unemployment insurance, an FDR New Deal program, is necessary to prop up "aggregate demand" during a recession asserting "the welfare state stabilizes capitalism." By ignoring what causes slumps in the first place, namely, the Federal Reserve's creation of money and manipulation of interest rates, she is firmly in the interventionist school of thought advocating government spending to deal with the destabilizing Federal Reserve policies that cause the boom-bust cycle.

Ghilarducci praises CEOs of companies that "have built successful businesses that are based on giving employees robust compensation packages." In a free market, management decides what the best way is to compensate employees to get the maximum productivity from them. The fact that not all companies have the same compensation packages means that there will be robust competition for quality workers. Thus, the free market for labor will tend to raise wages and benefits for workers who may have better opportunities in other firms. This is fundamental labor market economics, which you think an economics professor would understand. Nevertheless, Ghilarducci decries the lack of universal health-care coverage in America as a global outlier among developed countries. She concludes her brief overview with her observation "that all advanced countries are welfare states, and there are good reasons for that."

In a similar vein, Columbia University economist Jeffrey Sachs, writing in *Scientific American* (November 2006), "Welfare States beyond Ideology," dismisses F. A. Hayek's analysis (*The Road to Serfdom* 1944) that the welfare state would lead to less freedom for the general public. According to Sachs, however, the Nordic states have robust market-based economies and extensive social spending. However, it does cite one of the most important reasons a country can have a comprehensive welfare state and a robust economy really low taxes on capital. Capital is the foundation of a robust economy. Without capital investment in machinery, factories, transportation, etc., there can be no abundance of goods for consumers. And as long as there is a consensus among the people that a welfare state is desirable, the relatively heavy taxes the people pay is usually considered reasonable.

Rounding out the case for the welfare state from startling perspectives are Bruce Bartlett, who served in the Reagan and George H. W. Bush administrations and also was on the staff of the late Congressman Jack Kemp and libertarian Republican Congressman Ron Paul; Will Wilkinson, former program director at the Institute for Humane Studies, a longtime classical liberal organization and currently affiliated with the Niskanen Center in Washington DC; and Brink Lindsey, vice president and director of the open Society project at Niskanen Center.

Bartlett's thesis in his *New York Times* op-ed, "The Conservative Case for the Welfare State," (December 25, 2012) is that the American people overwhelmingly support Social Security, Medicare, Medicaid, and therefore it is foolish to abolish them or tinker with their current structure. Also, Bartlett hangs his hat, so to speak, on the research by University of California, Davis academic Peter Lindert that purports to show that the welfare state is not a hindrance to economic growth and provides an important safety net for Americans. Bartlett also summarizes the professor's findings: "There are huge efficiencies in providing pensions and health care publicly rather than privately. A main reason is that in a properly run welfare state, benefits are nearly universal, which eliminates vast amounts of administrative overhead necessary to decide who is entitled to benefits and who isn't, as is the case in America, and eliminates the disincentives to work resulting from benefit phase-outs."

Then Bartlett engages in some wishful thinking, namely, that American conservatives should support a national health insurance scheme, citing the relatively high per capita administrative costs in the United States vis-à-vis the single-payer system in Canada. He also points out that the American health system is not the best in the world based upon the cost and outcomes of medical care in the United States compared with other nations in Europe who have embraced a single-payer system or some other form of national health insurance.

Summing up his essay that the American people, especially conservatives, should demand a larger welfare state because the Nordic countries provide more benefits to the people and have a higher index of life satisfaction, Bartlett makes an egregious error, namely, comparing apples with oranges. The Nordic nations are relatively homogeneous demographically and smaller than most states in America. As the previous critics Scandinavian welfare states have pointed out social spending can be maintained for a length of time until the demographics catch up with the ability of the people to pay for all the entitlements. In addition, a nation's culture whether people "buy in" to the notion of a governments cradle-to-grave policies can last for decades without major opposition. However, a day of reckoning is always on the horizon. Inasmuch as Bartlett's essay was written eight years ago, the recent evidence by economists who have analyzed the welfare state experiments in Scandinavia and have shown that all is not well in countries that Bernie Sanders and others want us to emulate should cause him to reconsider his unwavering support for a larger American welfare state.

Meanwhile, two self-described libertarians, Will Wilkinson and Brink Lindsey, who are currently both vice presidents at the Niskanen Center in Washington DC, give it the old college try, in two separate essays, calling for libertarians to embrace the welfare state. Their flawed logic is unconvincing.

In describing the libertarian support for the welfare state "neo-classical liberalism," Wilkinson turns libertarianism on its head in his essay, "Libertarian Principles, Niskanen, and Welfare Policy" (March 29, 2016). Citing the work of Matt Zwolinski and John Tomasi, authors of *Brief History of Libertarianism*, Wilkinson points out that they believe "the libertarian nonaggression principle is false and/or vacuous." Moreover, he states, "there is nothing inherently unlibertarian about redistributive poverty relief, and that a guaranteed basic income might be a good *libertarian* idea" (emphasis in original).

Wilkinson's tortured logic, namely, that libertarianism is compatible with "social justice" is at best naive but more likely selling out to the current politically correct notion that welfare is untouchable. If self-described libertarians cannot defend the philosophical foundation of libertarianism, the notion that redistribution is compatible with libertarianism is intellectually bankrupt.

Brink Lindsey's August 9, 2017, essay, "Why Libertarians and Conservatives Should Stop Opposing the Welfare State," describes himself as a "liberaltarian" who believes "that in the world we live in, a robust welfare state is a necessary element of a healthy free society." If there ever was an oxymoron that could be used to teach students about a *non sequitur*, Lindsey's statement would take center stage. He continues by asserting, "I see overwhelming evidence that government social programs greatly improve outcomes in key dimensions of human welfare." In other words, if bank robbers distribute money to residents of the neighborhood that undoubtedly would improve "human welfare," would Lindsey then applaud the redistribution of income made by a private citizen to another citizen by coercive means? After all, there is no fundamental difference between a "democratic" redistribution of income or an involuntary redistribution of income, which is commonly known as theft, fraud, etc. He then makes a gross assumption, "I see no reason to think that there is any invisible hand that could guide the voluntary nonprofit sector toward matching or improving on the government's record. I therefore conclude that a purist libertarian program of severely reducing or completely zeroing out the welfare state would result in disastrous increases in human suffering." Evidence? Wow, got that. Voluntary exchange is uncertain; therefore, we need the heavy hand of the welfare state to take money from producers—and workers—to distribute the plunder to the less fortunate in society.

Lindsey is right on the money when he observes our "culture will need to change" to effect a substantial reduction in or abolition of the welfare state. He correctly points out the counterproductive fiscal and regulatory policies that redistribute income to agribusiness and corporate entities. Surprisingly, he decries so-called tax preferences, claiming they "are terrible social policy." A tax preference is nothing more than a tax cut, which both conservatives and libertarians should applaud, because it means business owners and workers get to keep more of their own income.

This self-described liberaltarian concludes his essay with a call to both libertarians and libertarian-ish conservatives "to improve the quality, effectiveness, and efficiency of the safety net." Lindsey is clearly on the mark when he points out, "healthcare offers a dramatic case in point, as prices for medical services today have been grossly inflated by government policies [e.g., occupational licensing, fee-for-service reimbursement schedules, and patent protection for pharmaceuticals]. Change those policies and the cost of Medicare, Medicaid and other government healthcare subsidies will decline."

Lindsay throws the gauntlet down in his last paragraph after pointing out the challenge issued by Richard Cornuelle in *Reclaiming the American Dream* (1968), who called for a vigorous "independent sector" to downsize or abolish the welfare state. Lindsey asserts that it has been "a failure of libertarian ideas" of the past half century to replace the welfare state with nongovernmental social services. He thus concludes his essay with this unwarranted assertion:

> I don't believe it is possible for the nonprofit sector to outperform government and protecting people from certain downside risks of life in a complex, highly urbanized, individualistic society. At the very least, though, it reveals a failure of effort. I would be happy for opponents of the welfare state to prove me wrong. But first they have to try.

Below, we will review some of the major critiques of the welfare state that go 170 back years. Although these classic critiques—some of which were written well before America's welfare state became as widespread as it has—did not provide a blueprint or road map for libertarians to articulate to replace the welfare state. In recent decades, however, libertarians have provided specific policies to replace social welfare spending with nonprofit solutions.

The next several chapters—how to create a universal medical care system based on free markets, nonprofits, and personal responsibility—take up Lindsay's challenge and shows why the current health-care policies of government are counterproductive and can be replaced relatively quickly to improve the quality and outcomes of medical services.

The Case Against the Welfare State

Critiques of the welfare state in this section begins with French author and legislator Frédéric Bastiat, whose classic pamphlet (1850), *The Law* (http://bastiat.org/en/the_law.html), should be familiar to all conservatives and libertarians, especially the most recent crop of self-styled "bleeding—heart libertarians." Bastiat observed that "the state is the great fiction by which everyone tries to live at the expense of everyone else." Bastiat's assertion is based on his eponymous description of a society that conforms to the basic principles of justice—ending legal plunder. What is legal plunder?

Bastiat identifies legal plunder, which advocates of the welfare state should embrace as self-described compassionate individuals: "See if the law takes from some persons what belongs to them, and gives it to other persons to whom it does not belong. See if the law benefits one citizen at the expense of another by doing what the citizen himself cannot do without committing a crime." Plunder, therefore, is in effect a violation of the law, "the collective organization of the individual right to self-defense." Bastiat then aims his powerful fusillade against the welfare state in the following paragraph.

> You say: "There are persons who have no money," and you turn to the law. But the law is not a breast that fills itself with milk. Nor are the lacteal veins of the law supplied with milk from a source outside the society. Nothing can enter the public treasury for the benefit of one citizen or one class unless other citizens and other classes

have been forced to send it in. If every person draws from the treasury the amount that he has put in it, it is true that the law then plunders nobody. But this procedure does nothing for the persons who have no money. It does not promote equality of income. The law can be an instrument of equalization only as it takes from some persons and gives to other persons. When the law does this, it is an instrument of plunder.

With this in mind, examine the protective tariffs, subsidies, guaranteed profits, guaranteed jobs, relief and welfare schemes, public education, progressive taxation, free credit, and public works. You will find that they are always based on legal plunder, organized injustice.

Bastiat thus argued that any deviation from a super minimalist government is a gross violation of an individual's right to enjoy the fruits of his labor and would not lead to a society of peace and harmony. Government, therefore, must not be an instrument of legal plunder because it violates every human being's right to life, liberty, and property. In other words, the welfare state, which is based on legal plunder, cannot be defended because the ends do not justify the means. The only legitimate transactions in society must be based on voluntary exchange.

In America, thirty-three years after the publication of *The Law*, Yale University sociology professor William Graham Sumner's *What Social Classes Owe to Each Other* (https://cdn.mises.org/What%20 Social%20Classes%20Owe%20Each%20Other_2.pdf)   (1883) appeared that addressed the fundamental question of every society, namely, what is the proper interpersonal relationships in a free society. Sumner's insights about the history of the human race, government policies, and social order permeate his 145-page treatise.

For example, Sumner identifies one form of legal plunder. "Persons and classes have sought to win possession of the power of the State in order to live luxuriously out of the earnings of others.

Autocracies, aristocracies, theocracies, and all other organizations for holding political power, have exhibited only the same line of action." Thus, he continues, that in a free state, "*each man is guaranteed the use of all his own powers exclusively for his own welfare*" (emphasis in original). And the acid test about any institution is "the degree to which they guarantee liberty." Sumner therefore asserts, "A free man in a free democracy has no duty whatever toward other men of the same rank and standing, except respect, courtesy, and good-will." Furthermore, Sumner observes, "In a free state everyman is held and expected to take care of himself and his family, to make no trouble for his neighbor, and to contribute his full share to public interest and common necessities." This passage can be construed quite simply as Sumner's defense of promoting the general welfare, not the specific welfare of any specific individual or group.

Sumner's defense of laissez-faire is not only a necessary condition for prosperity but a moral imperative for social harmony. In other words, Sumner asserts that if we lived in a world where people would mind their own business, everyone's happiness would be assured, which means everyone would be free to pursue their (peaceful) actions to achieve their goals. Moreover, "laissez-faire would not give us perfect happiness." Imperfect human beings cannot create a perfect world but free human beings cooperating with one another create commerce, industrialization, and prosperity. That has been the story of free people throughout the world.

Sumner takes on cronyism in no uncertain terms, and his current take could be applied to the welfare state as well. "The greatest social evil with which we have to contend his jobbery... Jobbery is any scheme, which aims to gain, not by the legitimate fruits of industry and enterprise, but by extorting from somebody a part of this product in the guise of some pre-attended industrial undertaking."

He therefore points out, "The plan of plundering each other produces nothing. It only wastes." Sumner highlights "The Forgotten Man" who pays the bills for cronyism, and the welfare state has a choice to make about whether whom to help or not in society. He points out that individual conscience should guide our actions toward individuals who are less fortunate or the least fortunate in society.

Furthermore, "we each owe it to the other to guarantee rights. Rights do not pertain to results, but only to *chances*... It cannot be said that each one has a right to have some property, because if one man had such a right some other man or men would be under a corresponding obligation to provide him with some property. Each has a right to acquire and possess property if he can."

The advocates of the welfare state must come to grips with the trenchant critiques of redistribution by both Bastiat and Sumner. The two authors summarized why the welfare state is incompatible with a free society and social harmony. If the proponents of a comprehensive welfare state believe they take the high moral ground, then they have to defend legal plunder as socially necessary and economically benign. Additional critiques of the welfare state below reveal how it undermines the very fabric of civilized society.

In the twentieth century, critiques of the welfare state span both sides of the Atlantic by economists, political scientists, historians, philosophers, and other academics. The popular press also was a venue for critics to voice their opposition to the growing welfare state of the 1930s and beyond.

Henry Hazlitt, editorial writer, columnist, and author, wrote a comprehensive demolition of interventionist policies in his 1969, *Man vs. the Welfare State* (https://mises.org/library/man-vs-welfare-state-0). Hazlitt skillfully attacks the assertion that government spending in general is preferable to people spending their own money.

> Some champions of ever greater governmental power and spending recognize... Like Prof. J. K. Galbraith, for instance,...invent the theory that taxpayers, left to themselves, spend the money they have earned very foolishly, and all sorts of trivialities and rubbish, and that only the bureaucrats, by first seizing it from them, will know how to spend it wisely.

The term that best describes economists, other academics, and public officials who have this mindset is sheer arrogance. Denying people the right to spend their own money other than, as Bastiat argued, to delegate to government the collective right of self-defense of the people is to begin the slippery slope toward widespread legal plunder.

Hazlitt is even more insightful when he describes the essence of the welfare state.

> In this state nobody pays for the education of his own children, but everybody pays for the education of everybody else's children. Nobody pays his own medical bills, but everybody pays everybody else's medical bills. Nobody helps his elderly parents but everybody else's elderly parents. Nobody provides for the contingency of his own unemployment, his own sickness, his own old age, but everybody provides for the unemployment, sickness, or old age of everybody else.

The best way to describe the welfare state is that it is a nexus of subsidies and cross subsidies. In a free society, individuals and families would be responsible for their own well-being. The social safety net would be their own savings, help from their family, and (voluntary) support of their neighbors.

The welfare state, the seemingly endless number of programs to improve the current and future financial conditions of individuals and families, is counterproductive because it creates dependency, moral hazard situations and less than optimal economic output, and ultimately is financially unsustainable. For example, Social Security, is paying out more in benefits than it receives in taxes annually. The so-called Social Security trust fund will be exhausted in the early part of the next decade. For beneficiaries to receive the promised benefits, taxes will have to be raised on workers while the federal government may decide to raise taxes and cut benefits given the number of retirees that will be dependent on monthly Social Security checks beginning in the 2030s.

No matter how welfare state advocates spin this, one of the cornerstones of the welfare state, it is, in reality, no more than an intergenerational chain letter more commonly called a Ponzi scheme.

When it comes to relieving poverty and providing medical care, Hazlitt does see a role for government, asserting that private charity cannot solve these issues completely. His example of a youngster in an automobile crash, who must be rushed to a hospital immediately, is an example of appropriate government intervention if a family does not have medical insurance. Chapters 2 and 3 will outline a plan for universal medical coverage, so Hazlitt's example would be irrelevant in America, where everyone would be covered for any medical emergency.

The Mises Institute published two additional critiques of the welfare state in the twenty-first century. One by Per Bylund, "How Welfare States Make Us Less Civilized" (https://mises.org/wire/how-welfare-states-make-us-less-civilized), highlights one of the glaring weaknesses of the economic redistribution of income, the essence of the modern democratic welfare state. According to Bylund, "market-based bonds" are severed, and the links between individuals weaken a community's economic relationships. So instead of serving their fellow human being within the marketplace, a portion of the community lives off the production of other people. For the past century, Bylund asserts civil society has been replaced by bureaucratic systems, reducing personal interactions whereby local residents learn about each other and develop bonds that increase social harmony. The welfare state instead creates tension and conflict because the recipients of government largesse do not have any incentive to become entrepreneurs/employees themselves and have very little direct connection with other producers except as consumers of the goods in services being produced without their input.

All is not well in the prototypical welfare state, Sweden. In "The Welfare State Is Tearing Sweden Apart" (Mises Wire, https://mises.org/wire/welfare-state-tearing-sweden-apart), Jon Nylander observes that the country's subsidies have increased migration of low-skilled individuals from Third World countries and placed a huge burden other Swedish people and has had a profound effect on its culture. He concludes his essay with this analysis:

> Sweden's rampant welfare state is sick to the core. And it must therefore be questioned to its core, perhaps even allowed to perish. It isn't immigrants on welfare that should be crushed; although certainly a lot of welfare recipients and rent-seekers, among them immigrants, would have a hard time during a transition before they can find productive roles in civil society, and will have to leave on their own accord. This is a crying shame—but Swedes have chosen the welfare state for everyone and therefore ultimately: no-one. Combined with euphoric virtue signalling it has been shown to have a profoundly detrimental effect to the fabric of civil society. And now we must pay the price, one way or the other.
>
> These dynamics are playing out with full force in Sweden today, and it is heartbreaking to watch.

In a similar vein, economist Joseph Salerno's brief note on Finland's welfare state should raise alarms throughout the world ("The Agony of the Welfare State, Finish Style," https://mises. org/wire/agony-welfare-state-finnish-style). Salerno points out an important demographic factor regarding welfare states, especially how it is unfolding in Finland. To maintain a welfare state, personal income taxes have to be relatively high to pay for all the spending. In Finland, for example, Salerno points out that people are not reproducing in sufficient numbers, so enough tax revenue comes into the state's coffers to pay for the generous benefits. The Finnish fertility rate has dropped to just over 1.5 per woman, "and the number of people under 20 years of age as a percentage of the working age population is the lowest among Nordic countries at less than 40%, down from 60% in 1970." He quotes a bank economist who observed,

"We have a large public sector and the system needs taxpayers in the future." In short, the Finnish welfare state has been depressing reproduction rates; hence, the needed tax revenue to sustain generous welfare benefits cannot keep pace. No amount of wishful thinking can alter the facts—welfare states do not last forever. If demographics are destiny, then the destiny of not only the Finnish welfare state but also all welfare states it is indeed bleak.

Civilization depends on peaceful cooperation among all members of society. The welfare state tends to do the opposite—that is, a constituency emerges for more government benefits, which only can occur if entrepreneurs and workers are plundered. In contrast to the welfare state, a market economy does not offer or provide any guarantees to entrepreneurs or workers that there businesses will survive and their jobs will not disappear. Nor does a market economy condone in any shape way or form plunder. The market economy, however, provides an important factor that creates prosperity—the opportunity that everyone will be free to pursue his or her self-interest peacefully.

The welfare state also undermines the most fundamental institution of civilization, the family, according to Vedran Vuk in his essay, "The Welfare State's Attack on the Family" (July 12, 2006). As the previous essay pointed out how the welfare state make society less civilized, Vuk raises one of the most important issues regarding the establishment of a welfare state and its impact on the family unit. Prior to the welfare state, parents took care of their children so that when they no longer worked, the children could help take care of them. In other words, Vuk explains that he has no responsibility to strangers he's never met but responsibility to his immediate family. The welfare state, he asserts, with such programs as Social Security and unemployment insurance removes personal responsibility and replaces it with dependency on the state—in effect "crowding out" our moral responsibility.

As a native of the former Yugoslavia, Vuk lived through "socialist poverty," but his family pull together in those difficult times. His paternal grandmother saved for thirty years to send his father to medical school—no government help, no student loans—and when she developed breast cancer, his father took care of her. Clearly, not every family will have a doctor to take care of the elderly, but Vuk's point is that there is a natural cohesion in families, which the welfare state overrides with a myriad of programs that create intergenerational dependencies for basic necessities. His conclusion, it is noteworthy: "Movement away from the welfare state is a movement toward better family values and better family cohesiveness. The death of the family is the life of the state."

Conclusion

The welfare state was not born out of "an immaculate conception"—that is, it did not arise organically as a spontaneous, voluntary response to the needs of the people. The hallmark of the welfare state is that involuntary means are appropriate to justify laudable ends, namely, helping individuals and families who are facing a myriad of issues, ranging from low or no income, homelessness, medical needs, and age-income security.

Charitable associations, on the other hand, were created and consistent with the culture that took root in America—the spirit of helping neighbors voluntarily. We will explore how the nonprofit sector in chapter four would play an important role in creating a free market medical care sector by providing services to Americans who are dependent on Medicaid.

Chapter 2

Restoring the Doctor-Patient Relationship with Free Markets and Essential Insurance

A generous health insurance policy more or less covers
everything from a sniffle to a heart transplant. It shouldn't.
An insurance policy that covers routine care isn't even
an insurance policy, properly speaking—it is a very
expensive pre-payment plan that jacks up premiums.

—John Steele Gordon

In a rational insurance world, people would pay out of
pocket for inexpensive services and rely on insurance
to pay for expenses that are large and rare.

—John C. Goodman

Consumers…buoyed by insurance plans and tax breaks,
have little idea how much they are really spending
and little incentive to know underlying costs.

—Joseph Walker

Only market reforms have the potential to reduce
our astronomical spending on healthcare. The
big problem is people may not be ready.

—Max Gulker

T he American people have been sold a bill of goods, namely, employer-based medical insurance as well as other policies that have inflated the cost of health care in the country. And what a bill it is: $3.6 trillion in 2018. To put this in perspective, in 1966, the first full year, both Medicare and Medicaid expenditures were operational, total medical expenditures were $46.1 billion (not adjusted for inflation) and reached $3.6 trillion in 2018, an increase by a factor of nearly eighty. In 1966, out-of-pocket expenses ($18.6 billion) and private health insurance ($10.3 billion) comprised 63 percent of total medical care spending. By 2018, that combined percentage declined to 10 percent or $375 billion. In short, medical care costs have shifted dramatically to third-party payers—insurance companies, Medicare, and Medicaid—while out-of-pocket costs on a relative basis have declined substantially.

More recently, *medical care inflation* has increased faster than all components of the CPI, except college tuition ("The Inflation Nightmare") in the first two decades of the twenty-first century (see figure 1). No wonder the American people are unhappy with the current system as insurance premiums keep rising, costs are being shifted from insurance companies to policyholders and taxpayers who while not feeling the sting directly with higher taxes have to foot the bill for the increasing costs of Medicare, Medicaid, and other government medical care programs.

In 2019, the National Health Expenditures compiled by the Centers for Medicare & Medicaid Services published the following data about the country's medical spending in 2018.

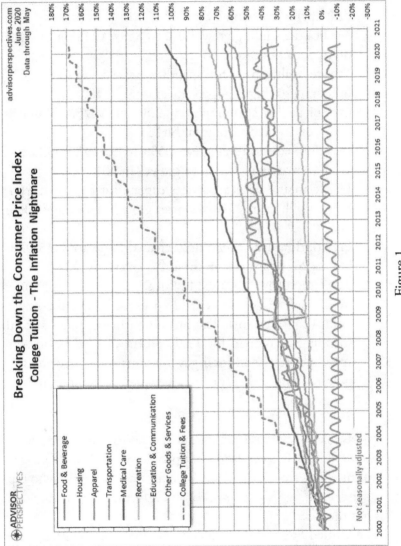

Figure 1

- NHE grew 4.6% to $3.6 trillion in 2018, or $11,172 per person, and accounted for 17.7% of Gross Domestic Product (GDP).
- Medicare spending grew 6.4% to $750.2 billion in 2018, or 21 percent of total NHE.
- Medicaid spending grew 3.0% to $597.4 billion in 2018, or 16 percent of total NHE.
- Private health insurance spending grew 5.8% to $1,243.0 billion in 2018, or 34 percent of total NHE.
- Out of pocket spending grew 2.8% to $375.6 billion in 2018, or 10 percent of total NHE.
- Hospital expenditures grew 4.5% to $1,191.8 billion in 2018, slower than the 4.7% growth in 2017.
- Physician and clinical services expenditures grew 4.1% to $725.6 billion in 2018, a slower growth than the 4.7% in 2017.
- Prescription drug spending increased 2.5% to $335.0 billion in 2018, faster than the 1.4% growth in 2017.
- The largest shares of total health spending were sponsored by the federal government (28.3 percent) and the households (28.4 percent). The private business share of health spending accounted for 19.9 percent of total health care spending, state and local governments accounted for 16.5 percent, and other private revenues accounted for 6.9 percent.

A reasonable conclusion from all the health-care spending in America would be that the American people would live longer and lead healthier lives than individuals from around the world who typically spend *no more than 13 percent* of GDP on medical care. But that is not the case.

The United States, by far, spends the most on medical/health care—private insurance, out-of-pocket expenses, hospitals, prescription drugs, physicians, and public programs, such as Medicare, Medicaid, and other taxpayer-funded expenditures—than any other major industrialized country. Yet despite the enormous amount of money that is spent on the health-care sector, the American people collectively are not as healthy as citizens of other nations that spend far less and have either a government single-payer system or some combination of mandated private insurance and government subsidies.

For example, in the thirty-six high-income countries that comprise the Organization for Economic and Cooperation and Development (OECD), the average annual national medical spending is 8.8 percent of GDP, *50 percent less than* in the United States. The countries include single-payer systems Canada (10.7 percent) and United Kingdom (9.8 percent) and Scandinavian countries, Sweden (11.0 percent) and Norway (10.2 percent), as well as both Germany and France (11.2 percent). These countries with different types of medical care systems typically have better health-care outcomes than the United States.

In the OECD, the average life expectancy is 80.7 years with Switzerland at the top of the list (83.6) while in the United States is 78.6 years with the other countries surpassing that of America. Drilling down into the US data, non-Hispanic Black Americans have an average life expectancy of 75.3 years; non-Hispanic Whites, 78.8 years; and Hispanic Americans, 81.8 years, similar to the life expectancy in the Netherlands, New Zealand, and Canada.

What helps explain the lower-life expectancy of US citizens vis-à-vis their counterparts in the OECD and the disparities in our country? One well-known metric is that 40 percent of the American population is obese compared with the 21 percent average in the OECD. Other countries obesity rates range from 32.2 percent in New Zealand to only 11.3 percent in Switzerland. Maybe living in a mountainous country where people hike, walk regularly, and ride bicycles is an important factor in staying lean and living longer. The Switzerland national anthem could, in fact, be the song popularized in both the movie and the play, *The Sound of Music*, "Climb Every Mountain." (In chapter 5, a discussion of wellness and personal responsibility will show how we can substantially lower medical costs.)

The effects of obesity on the American people's general health and the cost of health care cannot be underestimated. Chronic conditions related to obesity include diabetes, hypertension, heart disease, and cancer. And yet given the nation's medical care expenditures of $3.6 trillion, millions of Americans still are not treated or "undertreated" for their chronic conditions, leading to premature deaths, extensive emergency room visits and considerable hospital stays, and dependence on medications, all of which drive up the demand unnecessarily for medical care.

The United States' hybrid system of private expenditures and public funding of medical care is unsustainable in the very real sense that the nation's medical care costs are increasing faster than personal income. And with the graying of America, medical care costs will be accelerating in the decades ahead as the baby boomers will require more and possibly expensive treatment to deal with the inevitable aliment individuals face in their eighties and nineties. Moreover, according to numerous studies, America's medical care expenditures are inflated because of *unnecessary* insurance, waste,[1] and fraud that drain both the private sector and public sector of enormous amounts of money, and therefore, critics from across the political spectrum have proposed alternatives such as "Medicare for All" or "reforms" to lower the cost of medical care and improve the quality.

The projected National Health Expenditures, from 2019 to 2028, highlight the following:

- National health spending is projected to grow at an average annual rate of 5.4 percent for 2019–28 and to reach $6.2 trillion by 2028.
- Because national health expenditures are projected to grow 1.1 percentage points faster than gross domestic product per year on average over 2019–28, the health share of the

---

[1] One study estimates that as much as $935 billion is health-care spending is wasted annually. See William H. Shrank, Teresa L. Rogstad, and Natasha Parekh, "Waste in the US Health Care System: Estimated Costs and Potential for Savings," *JAMA*322, no. 15 (Oct. 7, 2019): 1501–9.

economy is projected to rise from 17.7 percent in 2018 to 19.7 percent in 2028.

- Price growth for medical goods and services (as measured by the personal health care deflator) is projected to accelerate, averaging 2.4 percent per year for 2019–28, partly reflecting faster expected growth in health sector wages.

- Among major payers, Medicare is expected to experience the fastest spending growth (7.6 percent per year over 2019–28), largely as a result of having the highest projected enrollment growth.

- The insured share of the population is expected to fall from 90.6 percent in 2018 to 89.4 percent by 2028.

The NHE outlook assumes no major structural changes in medical and health-care costs through the 2020s. If there were ever was a time for policymakers to put aside finger-pointing and hyper partisanship, it would be now. With tens of millions of Americans dependent on employer-sponsored medical insurance and virtually the rest of the population dependent on either Medicare and Medicaid to pay for most of their health-care costs, this chapter will review the objections to a free market medicine and outline how the free market can provide medical care, which would shrink substantially the Nation's astronomical nearly $4 trillion in health-care expenditures and improve the health of the American people.

However, contrary to the conventional view that more Americans need to be "insured" so that everyone has "access" to quality, affordable medical care, the American people are, in fact, "overinsured" and that a common sense, cost effective, and free market medical care is indeed feasible, realistic, and imperative.

The laws of economics and the principles of sound finance will achieve the goal of the Medicare for All advocates—low-cost, high-quality medical care for all American. In addition, the American people essentially have "outsourced" their medical decisions to insurance companies and taxpayer-funded programs like Medicare and Medicaid. This chapter will outline how a totally free market medical care approach would work for the more than 150 million Americans who are covered under an employer plan. Chapter 3 will recommend how senior citizens would no longer have to rely on Medicare to pay for their doctor bills, prescription drugs, and hospital stays. And the same goes for than the 70 million-plus Americans on Medicaid.

The Commonwealth Fund study, "US Healthcare From a Global Perspective, 2019: Higher Spending, Worse Outcomes" by Roosa Tikkanen and Melinda K. Abrams, concludes, "The US healthcare system is the most expensive in the world, but Americans continue to live relatively unhealthier and shorter lives than peers and other high-income countries. Efforts to rein in costs, improve affordability and access to medical needed care, coupled with greater effort to address risk factors, are required to alleviate the problem." The challenge we face in America, therefore, is to spend less on medical care, increase longevity of the American people, and reduce our chronic illnesses. Our hybrid system has created the current medical structure and the American people are paying for it to the tune of $3.6 trillion annually—and rising—and needlessly suffering from illnesses that could be mitigated and treated effectively with a *single-payer system that puts individuals in charge of their medical decisions instead of insurance companies and/or the federal government.*

So how did we get here? Why does the United States have the most expensive health-care system in the world with embarrassingly poor outcomes for a portion of the population?

Has there been insufficient government oversight, control, and funding of the medical sector, which has contributed to the relatively dismal health-care outcomes in America? Or are government intervention, overpriced medical insurance, and taxpayer funding of medical care counterproductive given our supposedly common values of freedom, financial independence, and voluntary community institutions to address the medical needs of low-income American individuals and families?

Historical Overview of Medicine and Insurance

The history of medical insurance is an example of how big government's good intentions (I know that's a stretch)—let's give policymakers the benefit of the doubt for a moment—to create Medicare, Medicaid, Obamacare, etc. has intruded in the lives of the American people and how it has *distorted one* of the most important fundamental relationship in society—the doctor-patient relationship. But it doesn't have to be that way. Nevertheless, *if current trends continue*, we will have a federal government "Medicare for All" sometime in the twenty-first century.

According to a May 2020 poll conducted by the Kaiser Family Foundation (KFF), there is broad "public support for more incremental changes to expand the public health insurance program in this country including proposals that expand the role of public programs like Medicare and Medicaid... And while partisans are divided on a Medicare-for-all national health plan, there is robust support among Democrats, and even support among over four in ten Republicans, for a government-run health plan, sometimes called a public option..."

There is an alternative to a public option or Medicare for All, which would in effect be a federal government run medical care program—a top-down approach to pay for health-care costs. Even if physicians do not become government employees and all hospitals are not nationalized in a government single-payer system, there would inevitably be more bureaucracy, ubiquitous "gatekeepers," widespread rationing, intolerable delays for tests and higher taxes to achieve an ideological goal—government "provided" universal medical care. However, we can have universal medical coverage, optimal well-being, and lower medical costs, which would not involve government in any way by tweaking the current hybrid system with free markets, not for ideological reasons but practical reasons. Markets deliver the goods and services people want. It would be no different when it comes to a free market medical system.

To understand how we are closer than ever before to a federal government universal medical care system, a brief historical overview of the practice of medicine and the creation of federal government programs reveals the incremental steps the federal government has taken to dominate and control the medical care sector over the past century.

Dale Steinreich recounts how the practice of medicine unfolded in America ("100 Years of Medical Robbery," https://mises.org/library/100-years-medical-robbery). Conventional medicine (allopathy) has come a long way since the mid-nineteenth century when physicians practiced bloodletting and injected patients with harmful ingredients such as mercury or antimony. Needless to say, the death rate from such "treatments" was unconscionable. Competing with so-called conventional medicine was eclecticism and homeopathy. The former stressed plant remedies, bed rest, and steam baths. The latter emphasized what most people consider prudent approaches to better health, such as a healthier diet, cleanliness, and reducing stress. Not surprisingly, the American people were skeptical of seeing a "mainstream" doctor for an illness.

Five years after the Civil War (1870), an estimated 62,000 physicians were treating patients in the United States. Out of the total 5,300 applied homeopathic techniques and 2,700 used eclectic measures to treat their patients. In addition, medical schools were mostly privately owned, and medical licensing was not required in most states.

Contrary to the accepted notion that nonconventional physicians and their "quackery" was causing widespread needless deaths from their "snake oil" remedies, the truth is so-called mainstream physicians were responsible for maiming and killing patients with the treatments noted above. Moreover, the American Medical Association (AMA) was founded in 1847 and was working with the Medical Society of New York to restrict entry into the profession with licensing laws and restricting the number of schools that trained eclectics and homeopaths. Ostensibly, the goal was to increase the standards of the medical profession, but the reality was to reduce competition so conventional allopaths would see their incomes rise while the supply of eclectics and homeopaths would decline.

And as an additional historical sidenote, the founder of the AMA, Nathan Smith Davis, was able (in 1870) to prohibit female and black physicians from obtaining membership in the organization. In short, racism and sexism even affected the medical profession.

As history has shown over and over again, many special interests work to feather their own nest at the expense of the public. By seeking government regulations to squash competition, in this case, reducing the number of individuals who would graduate from medical schools, which would in effect raise doctors' fees. But this is not the end of the story.

One of the most monumental events in the history of medicine occurred in the early twentieth century when the Carnegie Foundation hired Abraham Flexner at the behest of his brother Simon, who was serving as director of the Rockefeller Institute for Medical Research to head up the AMA's Council on Medical Education. What emerged was the Flexner report, which was essentially the AMA's unpublished 1906 report about the future of American medical schools. The report became a pretense for state medical boards and legislatures to begin closing medical schools, which effectively reduced the number of physicians entering the marketplace.

The Flexner report achieved its objective. The number of medical schools declined from 166 (in the early twentieth century) to 77 by the 1940s, and many rural schools were shut down, and only two African American schools remained open. Physicians' average annual incomes rose dramatically as well from about $600 in the mid-nineteenth century to more than $6,300 just before the Great Depression, which was about four times the average worker's salary.

Despite the relative primitive treatments by conventional physicians, progress in medical care was being made with the invention of the stethoscope in 1816, the opening of the first dental school in 1839, and the discovery of anesthesia in the 1840s. But one of the major breakthroughs occurred in the 1850s and '60s with the discovery that germs were the cause of infection and wounds during surgery. And with the development of vaccines in the late nineteenth century, the incidence of rabies fell dramatically, as well as such childhood illnesses as whooping cough and diphtheria. To put this in perspective, the death rate per one thousand children declined from 125.1 (1891) to 15.8 (1925). Life expectancy for adults also increased as the incidence of chronic illnesses—tuberculosis, pneumonia, and other deadly ailments at the time—declined dramatically.

Although tensions were building between conventionally trained physicians and so-called alternative practitioners, the American people spent very little on medical care. According to one study of families living in Columbus, Ohio, hospital care accounted for only 7.6 percent of medical expenditures. In fact, a 1919 study in the state of Illinois found that lost wages due to illness was the primary concern of families, not medical expenses. Thus, families were more interested in purchasing so-called sickness insurance, which would replace the breadwinner's income if he should become unable to work.

Commercial insurance companies were very much aligned with the general public regarding medical care insurance. In general, households wanted to be protected from loss of income and therefore joined fraternal societies, which were the primary organizations families joined to receive income while the breadwinner was recuperating. Insurance companies, on the other hand, concluded that "health" was not insurable because of adverse selection and moral hazard. People in poor health would prefer to have medical insurance while generally healthy people would not (adverse selection). In addition, people may tend to forgo healthy habits if they feel they will be protected from their own actions if they have medical insurance (moral hazard).

So given all the pushback for medical insurance in the country, how did insurance become such an integral part of the "health care" sector?

Some of the early examples of medical insurance (after the turn of the twentieth century) occurred in Oregon and Washington for timber and mining workers. To ensure that costs were contained while providing adequate medical care, adjusters scrutinized claims to make sure that fees were "reasonable" and procedures were necessary; hospital stays were also supervised closely. In Oregon, a physicians' group created their own plan to avoid the close monitoring by insurance company adjusters.

The very poor, mentally ill, or blind suffering from contagious diseases used hospitals prior to the twentieth century. In addition, hospitals were not known to be "healthy" institutions because germs were spread quite easily before antiseptic techniques became widespread. Hospitals proliferated from the late nineteenth century, numbering 149 to more than 7,000 a century later.

According to John Steele Gordon ("A Short History of Medical Insurance," https://imprimis.hillsdale.edu/short-history-american-medical-insurance/), prior to the 1920s, hospital insurance was unheard of until 1929 when 1,500 schoolteachers enrolled in a plan at a cost of six dollars per year that would provide them medical care at Baylor University Hospital with no more than twenty-one days of care. Hospitals now had a steady cash flow, which was in their financial interest because they had large overhead costs. Soon, other hospitals began offering similar plans and allowed subscribers choice of hospitals to be treated in. In 1932, first Blue Cross plan began operations in Sacramento, California.

Hospital "insurance" did not adhere to sound principles of insurance. Basically, these new insurance plans were essentially prepaid hospital payments instead of covering only catastrophic illnesses. Although there was a limit on payments to hospitals, given the state of medical technology at the time, these plans were first introduced in the 1930s, the cost of hospital stays were relatively manageable. Even for severe illness, the birth of a baby or a less traumatic medical stay, cost per diem was roughly the same. By the 1950s, however, major medical insurance kicked in which covered subscribers for a catastrophic illness. But rather than replacing the current hospital insurance plans, major medical policies supplemented them.

A major flaw in hospital insurance eventually became obvious. Illnesses could only be treated in a hospital even though an outpatient approach would have been just as effective in many cases. In addition, insurance companies paid for hospital bills—no matter the amount—because there was no incentive for the patient/subscriber to "shop" for an effective low-cost hospital stay if it wasn't an emergency procedure. Hospital insurance, therefore, insulated patients from high hospital costs, which virtually guaranteed robust cash flows for hospitals. In short, the fundamental law of economics, the law of supply and demand, was turned upside down because consumers of medical care became indifferent to costs. As we shall see, consumer indifference because of medical insurance is one of the major causes of historically spiraling medical costs.

Soon, the American Hospital Association (AHA) and the AMA lobbied state legislatures so the "Blues" could get regulatory relief; in turn, the Blues would accept all enrollees and operate as a nonprofit organization. The Internal Revenue Service concurred by granting the Blues tax-exempt status, classifying them as charitable organizations. As a charitable organization, substantial reserve funds were not required.

The tax-exempt, nonprofit structure of Blue Cross also benefited Blue Shield, which was created in the 1930s by physicians as another prepaid plan to make sure they would receive payment from patients during the Great Depression. Physicians and the AMA crafted guidelines so that voluntary medical insurance would not interfere with their practices and their incomes. Furthermore, physicians were able to charge patients the difference between their reimbursement and their customary fees under the Blue Shield umbrella. This allowed doctors the flexibility to "discriminate" among patients based upon their ability to pay.

Both Blue Cross and Blue Shield did not offer "real" insurance coverage; thus, the die was cast for the distortions in the medical sector for decades to come. Hospitals had no incentive to hold down expenses because they were paid on a cost-plus basis. Patients, as we have seen, were guilty of over consuming medical services because they were shielded from the cost of physician fees and other expenses. Especially egregious was the community rating premiums, which meant that healthy twenty- and thirty-year-old individuals would pay the same premium as older subscribers who typically incurred at least four times the medical expenses as younger policyholders. Lastly, without the need to have substantial reserves, the premiums collected only covered annual expenses, and rising premium costs became the norm as extraordinary costs would require higher premiums in future years.

But the major distortions that have occurred in medical care and the insurance sector for the past seven decades was a result of price controls enacted by the federal government during World War II. Employers could no longer compete with higher wages because of the wartime controls; thus, they offered health insurance policies to attract labor to fill positions. Now medical insurance was closely tied to employment. These benefits were tax-free to employers and tax-deductible to employers.

Instead of having a vibrant medical insurance market for individuals based upon sound actuarial principles, the American people became accustomed to having medical insurance provided by their employers. The ramifications of this World War II regulation has had profound impact on the structure of medical care in the United States, not the least of which is workers remaining on jobs they necessarily may not have wanted to stay in but because of generous health-care benefits, they stuck it out, so to speak.

The fallout from employer paid medical insurance is that the self-employed and small business owners found that insurance policies became prohibitive for individuals and for companies with fewer than twenty-five or fifty employees. So while the number of Americans who had employer paid medical insurance grew substantially in the post-World War II period, the number of uninsured also grew rapidly during this era, which eventually led to the passage of the Affordable Care Act also known as Obamacare in 2010. In addition, both Medicare and Medicaid became law in July 1965, which critics at the time saw as a threat to the practice of medicine and the doctor-patient relationship.

Free Market Insurance: Pros and Cons

The critics of free markets in medicine and insurance

In general, economists support a market economy because it is the best/optimal method to allocate scarce resources; in addition, a market economy provides opportunities for both producers and consumers to achieve their goals peacefully and voluntarily. A totally free market economy creates widespread prosperity for all members of society overtime. How?

Entrepreneurs invest in capital goods, which are used to produce the goods and services people desire. Overtime, prices gently fall thereby spreading the benefits of greater output of goods and services to the masses. This is the "natural" price deflation that occurred throughout most of the nineteenth century in America when government intervention was relatively minimal compared with current economic and monetary policies. Yet mistakes are made in a market economy when entrepreneurs misread consumers' desires and/or undertake projects that turn out to be unsustainable because of the Federal Reserve's inflationary/interest rate policies. Entrepreneurs then have to learn from their mistakes and produce more desirable goods and services or go out of business. Business owners and corporate executives are constantly "on trial" before the jury of their peers—consumers across the country—who vote with their dollars every day in the marketplace. Thus, there is no shortcut to rising living standards except by saving and investing in a free market.

The Austrian economist Ludwig von Mises summed up the efficacy of a market economy.

> The market economy is the social system of the division of labor under private ownership of the means of production. Everybody acts on his own behalf; but everybody's actions aim at the satisfaction of other people's needs as well as at the satisfaction of his own. Everybody in acting serves his fellow citizens.

Unfortunately, an unfettered market economy never existed in America. If it had, our standard of living would be much higher today. The evidence is overwhelming. The sheer waste of scarce resources, that is, the use of taxpayer funds to pay for what has been dubbed the welfare-warfare state—the redistribution of income from producers to non-producers such as the $22 trillion spent on Great Society programs since the 1960s and the huge military-industrial complex, which has built American military bases around the world and has been instrumental in planning and starting undeclared wars during the past hundred years—has made us poorer as a nation. And if we include the untold damage done to the economy by the Federal Reserve's manipulating interest rates, causing the boom-bust cycle since its inception in 1914, its first full year in operation, and despite all these unnecessary interventions, the US economy still has created substantial prosperity for the past century. The federal government's counterproductive tax-and-spend policies and the fed's intervention in the financial markets have taken their tolls on substantial portions of the country over time.

Legendary investor Warren Buffett, longtime CEO of Berkshire Hathaway, probably said it best regarding the resiliency of the US economy.

> Who has ever benefited during the past 237 years by betting against America? If you compare our country's present condition to that existing in 1776, you have to rub your eyes in wonder. And the dynamism embedded in our market economy will continue to work its magic. America's best days lie ahead.

Nevertheless, government interventions in the form of regulations, licensing, subsidies, tariffs, and, yes, taxes, all have been interfering with the voluntary choices of the people in all sectors of the economy since the early days of the Republic. There is probably no sector that has been more regulated than medical care. The previous section highlighted the incremental steps over more than one hundred years that has led to massive government intervention from physician licensing, insurance regulations, pharmaceutical industry oversight and drug approval, and the creation of Medicare, Medicaid, Obamacare, and other taxpayer-funded programs.

The American people's prosperity is no accident. It has been based on economic freedom. Without economic freedom, the desires of consumers would be undermined by bureaucratic decision-making. Our mixed economy so far has survived despite all the unnecessary regulations have heaped on the productive sectors. The great achievements of the past several decades in technology, medical supplies and equipment, telecommunications, and other sectors have been made possible by the creativity of individuals working in relatively free economies. The centrally planned economies have failed miserably in raising living standards of their peoples. Yet analysts in a numerous disciplines, as well as most public officials, have considered health care too important to be left to the free market. Why?

One of the foundations of government intervention in the medical sector is the notion that "health care is a right," and therefore, the federal government should guarantee that right with either a single-payer system (Canada or the United Kingdom) or what has been labeled Medicare for All. The idea that health care is a right misconstrues the notion of rights. This is the difference between so-called positive and negative rights. A positive right is based upon the idea that you are entitled something from the government—money, food, clothing, housing, medical care, etc. A negative right, on the other hand, is a constraint on government behavior against an individual.

The Bill of Rights, for example, acknowledges the fundamental (negative) rights of the American people that the government cannot interfere with. The enumerated rights do not mean that the government provides us with a printing press to exercise our free speech rights or houses of worship to practice our religion or a firearm to keep and bear arms. In fact, the Ninth Amendment clearly states that just because *a right is not enumerated* in the Constitution, the people don't have other rights, which are implied for citizens living in a free country. Presumably, that would include the right to make medical decisions without government intervention. Moreover, in Article II, Section 8 of the Constitution, the powers of Congress are spelled out quite specifically, and there is absolutely no authorization for the federal government to be involved in or interfere with the medical care decisions of the American people. However, the Supreme Court over the decades has allowed the federal government to intervene massively in the economy based upon the following clause in Section 8, regarding one of the powers of Congress, "To regulate commerce with foreign nations, and among the several states, and with the Indian tribes."

Modern-day constitutional scholars, jurists, and others, who have asserted that the federal government can "regulate" any economic activity between people in different states, have interpreted this clause literally—and mistakenly. That's precisely what's happened since at least the New Deal when FDR signed legislation giving the federal government widespread regulatory powers over virtually every sector over the economy. This begs the obvious question. Did the founders fight a revolution to break away from Britain so the federal government can effectively do to citizens of the new republic what the British crown did to the American colonists? To ask the question is to answer it. In other words, a free market, laissez-faire, economy reflects the principles of both the Declaration of Independence and the Bill of Rights.

So if health care is not "right" because in any transaction there must be a willing buyer *and* seller and there is nothing in our Constitution that supports positive rights, then medical care as well as other services people desire must be obtained in the marketplace to satisfy the principle of liberty and optimal allocation of resources.

Surgeon and public health researcher Atul Gawande, writing in the *New Yorker* ("Is Health Care A Right?" October 2, 2017), describes his visit to Athens, Ohio, where he grew up to discuss health care with friends and other residents. The good doctor asserts *that the* country needs "a basic system of health-care coverage that's open to all" and correct the "mistake" of the decision made during World War II to link health-care coverage with employment. This makes eminent sense. The question is, How does the country go from our hybrid system to universal coverage?

Gawande outlines the choices before us:

> Do we want a single, nationwide payer of
> care (Medicare for all), each state to have its own

payer of care (Medicaid for all), a nationwide marketplace where we all choose among a selection of health plans (Healthcare.gov for all), or personal accounts that we can use to pay directly for health care (Health Savings Accounts for all)? Any of these can work. Each has been made to work universally somewhere in the world. They all have their supporters and their opponents. We disagree about which benefits should be covered, how generous the financial protection should be, and how we should pay for it. We disagree, as well, about the trade-offs we will accept: for instance, between increasing simplicity and increasing choice; or between advancing innovation and reducing costs.

To claim that each of the four medical care systems he outlines "can work" and each one works "somewhere in the world" is incorrect. Three of the four choices outlined above depend upon government subsidies and regulations to make their medical care systems work in order to get us to universal medical coverage. In other words, medical care is too important to be left completely to individuals because they are not fully informed to make optimal medical decisions and/or do not have the means to pay for their medical expenses without government (taxpayers' subsidies). The American people have become so dependent upon employer-based medical coverage, Medicare, Medicaid, and other government programs they have to rely on third-party payers who have become the gatekeepers for their medical care.

No country has had a free market medical care system. As Avik Roy points out in his essay ("Bringing Private Health Insurance into the 21st Century," April 17, 2019), "No industrialized nation has a *libertarian* healthcare system in which the government plays no role in subsidizing or regulating health insurance." Most industrialized countries, however, have "market-based" models of private insurance and government subsidies. Even Roy, who can be described as a conservative, does not propose a free market medical system in analyzing the status quo, but a "market-based system" where there is more choice, consumer-driven incentives, greater access to doctors, reduction in costs, and fiscal sustainability. All worthwhile goals, which he believes the United States can attain by emulating Switzerland's health-care system.

The case against a free market medical system and its corollary a free market medical insurance marketplace rests on several dubious assertions and assumptions. Nobel Laureate in Economics Paul Krugman asserted in one of his *New York Times* columns ("Health Economics 101," November 14, 2005), "The free market doesn't work for health insurance and never did. All we ever had was a patchwork, semiprivate system supported by large government subsidies." His conclusion is based on the observation that "private markets for health insurance suffer from a severe case of the economic problem known as 'adverse selection,' in which bad risks drive out good." The reason Krugman gives for a free market medical insurance being untenable is that unhealthy people will be priced out of the marketplace because the cost to insure them would be relatively high—and thus unaffordable.

Healthy individuals would want a low-cost policy because they would need less medical care and would not want to pay for an insurance policy that in effect subsidies unhealthy policyholders. But unbeknownst to Krugman, he is highlighting one of the problems with our current medical insurance structure, namely, that people want to be a "free rider." If people live unhealthy lifestyles, that is, and are overweight, drink too much alcohol, smoke, etc., they will tend to have more illnesses than individuals who do what medical experts claim we should do to avoid or at least reduce our risk of illnesses—keep your weight down, drink moderately, if at all, don't smoke, exercise frequently, reduce stress, be productive, and get enough sleep. However, there are individuals who have been "dealt a bad hand" from birth or have a genetic disposition to illnesses. As we shall see further in this chapter, a new universal medical care system would cover everyone from in utero to end of life, and thus preexisting conditions would not be an issue for future generations.

Krugman's essay, although containing some grains of truth about medical insurance, asserts only government programs, such as Medicare and Medicaid (remember this was written five years before Obamacare was enacted), are in fact necessary to promote "social justice." More recently ("The Plot Against Healthcare Continues," *New York Times*, January 14, 2020), he opines that additional government subsidies would "improve both quality and quantity of coverage" without offering any evidence. Krugman essentially believes that government intervention in medical care with mandates and subsidies has been a net benefit to the previously uninsured in the country. While it's true that the number of uninsured in America has declined because of the Affordable Care Act, it is also true that the ACA has made medical insurance unaffordable for many self-employed Americans.

One New Jersey freelancer (TS) explained how he has been affected by the ACA in a recent e-mail. If TS's experience with the ACA is not that uncommon around the country, then Krugman and others should at least reconsider their unequivocal support for government intervention in medical insurance. Government intervention in medical care insurance to create a universal system is not based on sound economic principles but an untenable ideological goal.

What the Affordable Healthcare Act has done to me:

> This is a story of a worker that was economically ruined by The Affordable Healthcare Act. Graduating from The New School with a BFA and a G.P.A. of 3.8 was the start of a long a very and fulfilling career in graphics. The downturn of 2008 and ensuing long recession was tough enough to cause me financial hardship. To make matters worse when the Affordable Healthcare Act was enacted it mandated that anyone who worked 30 hours or more a week would be entitled to ACA benefits. This caused many employers to cut working hours to 29 hours a week or

to treat emergency room patients who face, in some cases, hundreds of thousand dollars in medical expenses they did not contract for.

Nahvi recounts his treatment of patients who have been admitted unconscious into the emergency room because they suffered substantial trauma from a car accident, an undiagnosed medical condition, or a mugging. He rightfully points out that the three patients he treated did not give consent to their medical treatments because they were unconscious even though he saved their lives. Based upon his experience, Nahvi states, "Deep down inside, we all intuitively know that healthcare is not a free market, or else society would not allow me to routinely care for people when they are in no position to make decisions for themselves." He then goes on to make the incredible statement, "If they [Republicans] want medicine to be truly free market, then they have to be willing to let the next man or woman defined lying unconscious in the street remained there and die. In a truly free market, we cannot treat someone—and charge someone—without their consent and against their will." Navi concludes his essay by calling for "a caring system that serves all people fairly."

Nahvi is correct on one salient point. In a free market, there must be "consent"—mutual agreement—between a willing buyer and a willing seller. So how does an individual give consent if he or she is brought to an emergency room unconscious? This piece of the puzzle, creating a comprehensive universal medical care system, will be discussed in the final section of this chapter; namely, how to provide emergency room medical insurance for all 330 million Americans so when anyone is transported to a hospital or other facility because of an accident, a life-threatening medical condition (heart attack, stroke, etc.) and need immediate lifesaving treatment? The cost of treatment must be paid. But how?

Can free market medical insurance provide for lifesaving medications like insulin so patients no longer have to hassle with their insurance companies, an experience that left Rachel Madley recount her ordeal ("Does Anyone Really Love Private Insurance?" *New York Times*, September 18, 2019) that nearly shortened her life at the age of fourteen when she nearly lapsed into a diabetic coma from an undiagnosed Type 1 diabetes condition. One time in college, she was in dire straits because the insurance company office was closed and could not get a prescription. The local pharmacist provided her the insulin even though she did not have the required prescription.

Madley, who is identified as a student board member of the New York chapter of Physicians for a National Health Program and a PhD student at Columbia University Medical Center, calls for a "single-payer version of 'Medicare for all,' in which care is publicly funded by one entity and privately delivered, [that] would guarantee coverage to everyone in the United States, and eliminate the greed and administrative waste of private insurance." She concludes her essay with the observation that undoubtedly resonates with the substantial number of individuals and families who struggle to pay for health care. "I know I'll never live a day without worrying about my health. But maybe one day I, and millions of other diabetics in America, can live without worrying about how to pay for it."

Madley's "nightmarish relationship with the insurance industry" that began thirteen years ago has caused her to advocate for single-payer system. Instead of analyzing how a free market medical insurance could address her needs and those of millions of other Americans who suffer chronic conditions, she opts for a simplistic solution, turning over medical decision-making—and funding—to the federal government in the belief that everyone in America would receive the medical care and/or medication they need to lead healthy lives. Is a single-payer system the panacea she thinks it is?

According to Lee Kurisko, a Canadian-trained radiologist and currently practicing in Minnesota, is the author of *Health Reform: The End of the American Revolution?* (Alethos Press LLC, 2009) and has penned several articles about the flaws in Canada's single-payer system. In an essay he co-authored in 2009 with Dave Racer for the *Journal of American Physicians and Surgeons*, "What America Needs to Learn from Canadian Medicare," they provide several "lessons" for America that highlight why a single-payer system is counterproductive and do not provide the best outcomes for patients.

The first lesson is central planning does not work. Kurisko's personal experience with the shortcomings Canadian treatment occurred when his brother was in a hospital needing an MRI to diag-

nose a life-threatening illness during Christmastime.[2] Although anyone could make a purchase in the hospital coffee shop, where people
could spend their own money on what they wanted, the hospital did
not allow an MRI after 5:00 p.m. on weekdays and on weekends and
holidays even if patients wanted to pay out of pocket for the service.
Canadian hospitals are given budget by the government and cannot
exceed it. Kurisko concluded that centralized medical decision-making does not meet patient's needs, but a medical marketplace would
allow patients and doctors to agree on a mutually acceptable price
for services.

Kurisko's second lesson should be familiar to all economists
and anyone who lived through the 1970s in America: price controls
do not work. Price controls cause shortages especially in the supply
of family physicians. In the US "arbitrary Medicare fee schedules"
exacerbate the dearth of family physicians relative to specialists who
typically earn more.

Kurisko's lesson three is one that is ignored by advocates of
the single-payer system: "whoever controls the dollars is boss." He
describes how he was doing a procedure on a patient with the twelve-
year-old machine that was "outdated and clunky." During the procedure where he threaded a catheter from the patient's femoral artery
into the internal carotid artery, the risk of stroke increased substantially when the machine failed. When the technologist assisting him
got the unit to work, Dr. Kuriskco was relieved, and the anxiety he
faced during the procedure abated. After seeking legal counsel, he
told his superior that he was going to inform patients the risk they
faced because he was using "such dangerous equipment." Not surprisingly, the hospital soon received the new equipment after the threat
of legal ramifications by continuing to use such shoddy equipment.

---

[2] Dr. Kurisko chronicles his brother's illness—and the unconscionable delay
in getting an MRI and the several misdiagnoses over many months for what
turned out to be an advanced stage nasopharyngeal cancer—in an essay,
"Health Care—A Tale of Two Countries," *MetroDoctors*, July/August 2005. In
a recent e-mail, he pointed out his sister will get a knee replacement in a year
because there is a shortage of surgeons and strict budget constraints in Canada's
single-payer system.

Kurisko's experience in the centralized, bureaucratic Canadian health-care system was an eye-opener for him. He thought his country's single-payer system was the best way to provide medical care for the thirty million people Canadians. The reality of a single-payer system forced him to rethink his support for collectivized medical care system. At the end of this lesson, he offers suggestions, which will be incorporated in this chapter to create a free market universal medical system in the United States.

The final Kurisko lesson that will be presented here has to do with the Canadian culture and how it has impacted their medical care. According to Kurisko, Canadians have accepted the interminable wait for medical tests and procedures, which he believes would be unacceptable in the United States. Why? Canadians believe their medical care is "free" even though the taxes they pay are "exorbitant" and have accepted long waits as a trade-off for their universal coverage. He also believes Canadians are more "passive" than Americans when it comes to public policies they may disagree with while Americans tend to be more rambunctious than their northern neighbors if they dislike a public policy. As a physician in the United States, after having become disillusioned with the Canadian medical care system, Kurisko believes the American people could "be seduced" with the promise of "free" universal medical care funded by the federal government if Obamacare morphs into a single-payer system. Kurisko, thus, has become a passionate advocate of free market medicine and a critic of third-party payers, as evidenced by his book and articles, which reveal the shortcomings of government meddling in medicine.

The road map to free market insurance and medicine

This section will outline several steps that would be implemented to restore the doctor-patient relationship for the more than 150 million Americans who have employer-based medical coverage. The next chapter will review how Medicare, Medicaid, and Obamacare could also be replaced with free market medical insurance and coverage, which would be the last piece of the puzzle to create a universal medical care system from conception to end of life.

The single-payer system that would emerge from the current hybrid approach of providing medical coverage could reduce the nation's nearly $4 trillion annual medical costs by 50 percent or more. By substituting a free market in both medicine and insurance, massive government subsidies and overpriced individual and employer insurance policies would be assigned to the dustbin of history. A new era in the restoration of the American people's freedom of choice in medical care will begin.

Less than a year before the Affordable Care Act, more popularly known as Obamacare, was passed in March 2010, economist and libertarian philosopher Hans-Hermann Hoppe wrote a brief essay, "A Four Step Healthcare Solution" (Mises.org, August 14, 2009), outlining what a pure free market medical system would look like.

1. *Eliminate all licensing requirements for medical schools, hospitals, pharmacies, medical doctors, and other health-care personnel. Their supply would almost instantly increase, prices would fall, and a greater variety of health-care services would appear on the market.*

2. *Eliminate all government restrictions on the production and sale of pharmaceutical products and medical devices. This means no more Food and Drug Administration, which presently hinders innovation and increases costs.*

3. *Deregulate the health-insurance industry. Private enterprise can offer insurance against events over whose outcome the insured possesses no control. One cannot insure oneself against suicide or bankruptcy, for example, because it is in one's own hands to bring these events about.*

4. *Eliminate all subsidies to the sick or unhealthy. Subsidies create more of whatever is being subsidized. Subsidies for the ill and diseased promote carelessness, indigence, and dependency. If we eliminate such subsidies, we would strengthen the will to live healthy lives and to work for a living. In the first instance, that means abolishing Medicare and Medicaid.*

Hoppe's justification for each of his four proposals is based on a fundamental premise, namely, that in a free society, individuals and institutions are responsible for their actions; the people are entitled to make their medical decisions without government interference; and everyone including physicians, hospitals, insurance companies, medical suppliers, and pharmaceutical companies must be held accountable for their behavior. In addition, in a free market, prices must be transparent. This would increase competition and thus lower prices for all medical needs.

Some—if not the overwhelming number of Americans—would find Hoppe's four solutions untenable and therefore impracticable and possibly even dangerous because the people and medical providers have become used to government oversight and interference in the health-care sector to protect us from unsafe drugs, unproven medical procedures, and "price gouging." Moreover, inasmuch as a substantial number of Americans believe "health care is a right," it is inconceivable to them that a free market for medical care would even be desirable. The following analysis will provide the evidence for free market health-care system and focus on Hoppe's third solution, deregulating the health insurance industry.

The country's employer-based medical insurance coverage is yet another example how government intervention, in this case, wage and price controls during World War II, has distorted the economy. When the federal government permitted employers to deduct health insurance premiums as a tax-deductible expense and provide a tax-free benefit for employees, overtime, employers had a greater incentive as well as employees to want more medical coverage instead of higher wages and salaries. The inevitable result of this quirk in the tax code increased the demand for health insurance. In addition, state governments, which regulate the types of policies that can be offered to the employers and individual policyholders, mandated more and more coverage; insurance premiums have skyrocketed over the decades.

As Hoppe points out in his essay, "Because a person's health, or lack of it, lies increasingly within his own control, many, if not most health risks, are actually uninsurable." This is the conundrum of

American health care—insurance companies being forced to pay for "uninsurable" goods and services that should be paid for by individuals out of pocket. This would dramatically reduce health insurance premiums for all Americans. The objection to this, of course, is that people cannot afford to pay for necessary equipment and services. As we shall see, instead of employers and individuals and families paying exorbitant health insurance premiums, the freed-up dollars would be able to pay for most, if not all, these goods and services. In addition, in chapter 4, we will see how the nonprofit health-care sector would pay a greater role in providing medical care to low-income individuals and families.

As Ralph Weber (with Dave Racer), author of *Rigged: How Insurance Ruined Healthcare: (and how to fix it)*, and founder of MediBid.com, points out in his comprehensive (critical) review of the insurance industry, Medicare, Medicaid, and Obamacare, lobbyists and other special interest groups continually flood legislators at the state and federal levels with requests for insurance companies to cover such *(noninsurable)* items as in vitro treatments, wigs, wheelchairs, and a host of other goods and services. Couples, cancer patients, and the disabled undoubtedly desire these goods and services to improve their lives. But there is a huge cost to our society in trying to insure virtually every health and medical need. There are however less costly alternatives. Let's explore them.

Traditional employer-based insurance is a high-premium policy, typically with co-pays, deductibles, and possibly out-of-pocket expenses. Employees and if they have dependents, such as a spouse and/or children, cost employers $20,000 or more per family policy. For single, individual employees, the cost of such a policy could be at least $10,000 annually. The coverage typically includes doctors' visits, consultation/treatment with specialists and hospital stays, as well as medication. Under the current insurance coverage arrangement, patients do not get a bill, but the physician, hospital, pharmacy, etc. are reimbursed by the insurance company. Physicians, depending upon the size of the practice, and hospitals typically need to have, in many cases, a large clerical staff to file claims with the numerous insurance companies they are associated with. For physicians to maximize the revenue for their practice, they tend to spend anywhere from ten to twenty minutes per patient. For most physicians, they have about two thousand patients in their practice. Is this the best practice for the medical profession and patients?

There is a better way to treat patients for common ailments according to physicians David Cunningham and Rebekah Bernard who practice in Massachusetts and Florida, respectively. Both physicians were in traditional practices dealing with insurance companies, long hours, and spending less and less time with their patients and concluded they were doing a disservice to their patients. Consequently, they now became part of a growing trend in family medicine, *direct primary care*.

Direct primary care (DPC) is based upon a simple model by eliminating the middleman—the insurance company. Patients pay a monthly fee for access to doctors virtually 24-7. The benefits of DPC, according to Dr. Cunningham's website (Infinityfamilycare. com), include the following: "less unnecessary medication, fewer specialty referrals, less need for expensive testing, savings on labs and imaging fewer emergency and hospital visits, less waiting and frustration to talk to your doctor," which all lead to "happier patients!"

A DPC practice is primarily focused on preventing illnesses, modifying unhealthy lifestyles, providing necessary screenings, and working with patients to improve their wellness. In a DPC practice, a physician tends to have no more than six hundred to seven hundred patients, allowing him or her to spend upward of forty-five minutes and possibly as long as an hour during an office visit. Most office visits tend to be between thirty and forty-five minutes. And if the patient has to see a specialist, the DPC doctor has a referral network to tap into. For example, at Infinity Family Care, Dr. Cunningham uses a virtual referral service called Rubicon MD, which provides access to world-renowned specialists throughout the country.

In Dr. Bernard's practice, she maintains a list of local physicians and acts as an ombudsman for her patients, who tend not to have traditional medical insurance and thus pay cash for visiting a specialist. Recently, Dr. Bernard was able to help a patient get a back operation who did not have medical insurance. He was quoted

$20,000 at a local hospital. Dr. Bernard called the Surgery Center of Oklahoma (Surgerycenterok.com) for the patient who was able to have the operation for $5,000, which included transportation from Southwest Florida and other expenses. A 75 percent discount! The Surgery Center is also a cash-only practice that operates under free market model and has an enviable safety record and provides high-quality medical procedures.

The fee structure at Infinity Family Care is posted on its website, revealing the relatively modest fee for an individual and family.

Individual	$110/month
Couple	$200/month
Homebound patients	$250/month
Family Maximum	$350/month for up to two adults and their dependent children

NOTE: There is a onetime enrollment fee of *$75 per individual* and *$150 per family*. Minimum membership length is three months.

The following services are included in the monthly membership fee, which are outlined on the website, as well as the benefits are highlighted of being in a DPC practice for college students, young professionals, growing families, midlifers, and senior citizens.

Child wellness visits with all required vaccinations
- Adult health maintenance visits to review vaccinations, lifestyle, and recommended screenings, such as dermatology, and cardiovascular risk assessments
- Women's health care including cancer screening and IUD or Nexplanon insertion (cost of IUD or Nexplanon is additional but covered by insurance)
- Men's health care—including managing low testosterone and metabolic syndrome
- Advocacy—navigate and coordinate your care in a complex system

- Sick visits for everything from ingrown toenails to pneumonia
- Complex care management for chronic diseases such as diabetes and hypertension
- Preoperative and work physicals with EKG testing when appropriate—at no additional charge
- Camp, sports, and, in the very near future, DOT license exams
- Skin procedures such as mole biopsies and removal
- Orthopedic procedures including injections for painful knees and shoulders
- In-office testing for cholesterol, blood sugar, and Coumadin levels
- Prompt prescription renewals and follow-up on labs and test results

Infinity Primary Care lists the benefits for employers such as the estimated reduction in employee insurance costs by 20 percent. The benefits to employers also include the following:

- Savings on insurance costs
- Fewer sick days
- Less time away from work
- Fewer ER and hospital visits
- Savings on labs, imaging, medications
- No co-pays or deductibles

Infinity Family Care's pitch to employers is straightforward. "In the Direct Primary Care model *employers* pay a fixed monthly cost per employee [monthly membership] to Infinity and buy lowered premiums for an affordable high deductible insurance plan [for non-primary care]."

The current employer-based insurance coverage model is expensive and bureaucratic with insurance companies "interfering" in the doctor-patient relationship. By not having to file insurance claims, Infinity Care Model has two staffers assisting Drs. Cunningham and Cohen, which keeps their overhead costs at a minimum, allowing them to keep their membership fees reasonable. And patients have posted nearly two hundred glowing reviews of Infinity Family Care, https://www.infinityfamilycare.com/reviews/.

At Gulf Coast Direct Primary Care, Dr. Rebekah Bernard and her new associate Dr. Tameca Bakker provide similar services as Infinity Family Care (Gulfcoastdirectoryprimarycare.com), and the pricing schedule reflects the relatively lower income of Southwest Florida residents. Gulf Coast only has one assistant handling day-to-day administrative duties.

Children (up to 19): $39/month

Patients up to age 49: $69/month

Patients 50–64: $84/month

Patients 65+: $109/month

*Onetime registration fee of $250
* 10% discount offered for one-year payment or with ACH bank draft payments*

The pricing schedule at Gulf Coast reflects a simple proposition regarding medical care. As human beings age, they tend to require more medical care and thus more doctors' visits. Gulf Coast thus charges a higher membership fee for seniors than younger demographic groups. A couple with two children under nineteen would be charged $78, plus $138 for total of $216 per month, to obtain direct primary care at the Fort Myers Florida office. The annual cost for the family of four would be $2,592.

Gulf Coast provides medications at wholesale prices and searches GoodRX.com to obtain the lowest possible prices for its patients. DPCs are in effect a one-stop destination for individuals, couples, and families who want to escape the traditional employer-based insurance coverage and have a more "personalized" office visit experience an access to a primary care doctor virtually 24-7.

The first component of a single-payer system could be the establishment of Direct Primary Care practices throughout the United

States that would allow the more than 150 million Americans covered under employer-based insurance coverage to receive primary care without the middleman, an insurance company. This would require all internists and family physicians to transform their practices to a Direct Primary Care model. This is easier said than done because, currently, there are approximately only 1,200 DPC practices serving slightly more than 300,000 American patients. The United States would need between 215,000 to 250,000 physicians, each of whom would have approximately six hundred to seven hundred patients as an optimal number to make this model viable. Could it be done?

According to the Kaiser Family Foundation (KKF), in 2019, as reported in the Professionally Active Primary Care Physicians by Field table, there were nearly 200,000 internal medicine physicians and another 141,000 physicians in family medicine / general practice. There are currently enough physicians practicing that would make direct primary care a viable alternative to the traditional HMO, PPO or other arrangement that ties primary care with medical insurance.

The benefits for physicians under Direct Primary Care model are numerous: reduced patient load from approximately two thousand to between six hundred and seven hundred, lower overhead as support staff is eliminated, ending disputes with insurance companies, and probably greater satisfaction in their practices because they would be able to spend more time with their patients and they currently do leading to an increase inpatient wellness. Moreover, membership fees provide a steady cash flow, which could be equal to or greater than their current income. Even if their incomes decline as a DPC physician, their burnout rate would decline as well. Thus, for some (many?) physicians, the trade-off between a slightly lower income and reducing the stress of the current system may be well worth it.

The learning curve for physicians would have to be accelerated rapidly for their practices to embrace the Direct Primary Care model. Physicians would be entering an "unknown" territory in practicing medicine and would be wary of giving up their current "security" as a traditional fee-for-service associated with numerous insurance companies. Nevertheless, DPC physicians have a high level of satisfaction both professionally and financially—goals other physicians should explore so that the first piece of a single-payer system with the individual in charge and restoring of the doctor-patient relationship by eliminating the middleman can expand exponentially.

Even if a small number of physicians create DPC practices, they still could continue to be a fee-for-service practice and rely on patients who would not be reimbursed by an insurance company. John Steele Gordon's opening chapter quote must be implemented—eliminating insurance for routine care, which would lead to greater competition, transparent pricing, and lower office or virtual visit fees.

Other primary care approaches

Forward (Goforward.com) is a San Francisco-based health-care organization that "combines top-rated doctors with advanced technology to deeply understand your health today and build plans for your future" in order to provide personalized, preventative care. With offices in Los Angeles, New York, Washington DC, the San Francisco Bay Area, San Diego, and Orange County, California, Forward provides primary care in their offices or at home. The $149 monthly membership fee includes unlimited visits, biometric monitoring, labs and genetic analysis, and 24-7 messaging.

In many ways, Forward is similar to a Direct Primary Care practice. There are no co-pays or unexpected bills and a member works with a primary care doctor to develop a plan for optimal health outcomes. If necessary, Forward will refer patients to a specialist in their insurer's network. Each office has a team of physicians, which allows them to "scale up" the practice with more patients than are treated in a typical DPC office.

Forward has an impressive number of high-tech tools to diagnose an individual's baseline health metrics. According to founder and CEO Adrian Aoun,

> **We built a system to give our doctors superpowers.** They use software that integrates all your data—from genetics, to blood testing,

to sensors at home—to help you proactively instead of waiting for issues to arise. They spend more time with you because we built systems to handle their administrative tasks for them. They look at more risk factors because we automated many common tests and procedures. They make smarter decisions because we built algorithms and A.I. to tie those decisions to data. (Emphasis in the original)

As we will see in the wellness chapter, many illnesses are preventable. Forward's model is geared to providing its members with the information needed to optimize their health and thus reduce major medical expenses and hence the Nation's health-care expenditures.

VillageMD (Villagemd.com) was founded in 2013 by Tim Barry, CEO, Dr. Clyde Fields, chief medical officer, and Paul Martino, chief growth officer. Its mission is to provide primary care "anchored around the physician—patient relationship," using proprietary technology in order to manage the patients' needs based on a fee-for-service model. Any addition to physicians at their freestanding clinics, VillageMD partners within independent physicians and health-care systems to help transform medical care based on its model of value-based care.

Not only is medical care provided in freestanding clinics but also, in 2019, VillageMD began providing care at select Walgreens locations in Houston, Texas. In July 2020, VillageMD announced it would open between five hundred to seven hundred clinics at Walgreens pharmacies throughout the country over the next five years. The medical startup will receive $1 billion from Walgreens in equity and debt in exchange for a 30 percent stake in the company.

Although VillageMD has many characteristics of a DPC practice, there is no information on its website regarding its fee structure or schedule. Thus, there is no way of knowing if patients would still have to rely on insurance for reimbursement as a VillageMD patient or would have to pay out of pocket similar to a DPC practice. In any event, VillageMD could be another alternative to traditional employer-based insurance for employees to receive primary care.

CVS MinuteClinic is an initiative of CVS Pharmacies and is staffed by family nurse practitioners and physicians' assistants. According to the website, the health-care provides can "diagnose and treat common illnesses, injuries and skin conditions; administer vaccinations, screenings and physicals; write prescriptions when medically appropriate and provide patient education and recommendations. No appointment is needed but highly recommended at a Clinic, where dozens of medical services are provided (https://www.cvs.com/minuteclinic/clinic-visit), which can be paid in cash; the Clinic accepts payment by most insurance companies. Prices for the services are posted on the webpage, https://www.cvs.com/minuteclinic/insurance-and-billing. Video consultations are available 24/7 in most states for $59."

Eliminating insurance coverage for routine services would make the CVS MinuteClinic conform to the single-payer model advocated here—no insurance is needed to pay for routine medical care. Whether CVS would no longer accept insurance at its clinics would remain to be seen. The benefits to employees who have employer-based insurance and their employers would be substantial. Employers could deposit the current premiums in a health savings account (discussed in the next section) and employees would have to determine the most effective primary care for themselves and/or family. Self-employed individuals or employees who do not have traditional medical insurance and who want relatively low-cost primary care would have to their "homework" to determine what medical care they want. In other words, choice and competition would finally be the foundation of primary care without insurance, as the providers compete on price and quality.

Walmart opened its first "Walmart Health" center in Dallas, Georgia (September 2019), supplementing the nearly two dozen "Care Clinics" that had been opened in Georgia, South Carolina, and Texas. The services at Walmart Health (https://corporate.walmart.com/walmarthealth) include primary care, dental, counseling, labs and X-rays, health screening, fitness and nutrition, and health insurance education enrollment, all within ten thousand square feet in the Supercenter. According to Walmart's press release, September 13, 2019,

> The Walmart Health center will offer low, transparent pricing for key health services to provide great care at a great value, regardless of insurance coverage. Customers will be notified on the estimated cost of their visit when they book their appointment.
>
> The Walmart Health center will be operated by qualified medical professionals, including physicians, nurse practitioners, dentists, behavioral health providers, and optometrists. Walmart Care Hosts and Community Health Workers onsite will help customers navigate their visit, understand resources and be a familiar presence for regular visits.
>
> Working in partnership with wellness organizations, the Health center will offer specialized community health resources, online education and in-center workshops to educate the community about preventive health and wellness.

The Walmart Health center is another example, to some extent, of a "disrupter" to the traditional physician office visit paid for by an insurance company. However, the health center FAQ page (https://corporate.walmart.com/walmarthealth/faqs) highlight the business practices, which include having a relationship with one physician, who are contracted with Walmart, accepting insurance payments, and providing transparent pricing, to name a few of the center's organizational structure.

One possible drawback to the doctor-patient relationship at Walmart Health is turnover of the physicians who are on contract. As a new venture, it is too early to tell if this approach is sustainable.

Nevertheless, in the single-payer system, medical insurance would also be eliminated for Walmart Health center patients. Walmart asserts it "is committed to making health care more affordable and accessible for customers in the communities we serve." In a single-payer system, then Walmart Health should be able to deliver medical care even if no insurance for routine visits would be available.

One additional approach to primary care and other medical expenses that has gained popularity in recent years is a so-called health-sharing ministry, founded on faith-based principles. However, not all expenses are covered, inasmuch as the "Ministry" requires its members to lead healthy lifestyles in order to reduce major illnesses and thus keep annual fees relatively low. In many ways, a health-sharing organization is similar to a mutual aid society that David Beito chronicles in *From Mutual Aid to the Welfare State*. Thus, voluntary arrangements to share medical expenses would bloom if traditional insurance would be phased out and replaced by individual payment of primary care and other expenses.

Finance professional Jake Thorkildsen provides a comprehensive overview of health-care sharing versus traditional insurance in the following post, https://www.kitces.com/blog/healthcare-sharing-program-review-chm-medicare-lhs-samaritan-health-share-plans/.

In sum, the doctor-patient relationship can be restored under single-payer system using any of the approaches outlined above: Direct Primary Care practice, traditional fee-for-service with the patient's current physician, or being treated in a Forward health center, in a VillageMD clinic, a Walmart Health Center, or CVS Minute Clinic. To fulfill the requirements that insurance is not needed for routine visits, lab tests and other medical services, patients would pay out-of-pocket using cash or funds from their health savings accounts. At this point the savings to employers and individuals are incalculable, because all medical care providers would have to lower their prices in order to meet patients' ability to pay.

Health Savings Accounts

The second component of a single-payer system is establishing health savings accounts for all individuals who currently receive employer-based medical insurance. An HSA would be used to pay for virtually all medical expenses not related to direct primary care, such as an office visit with a specialist (e.g., cardiologist, neurologist, gastroenterologist, ophthalmologist, urologist, etc.) have a medical procedure such as a colonoscopy or biopsy that needs to be done in a clinic or hospital or any other expense that is typically not "routine." The HSA could also pay for an abortion, birth control pills, in vitro procedures, cosmetic surgery, and other medical/health-care expenses.

Another major benefit of an HSA is the "depoliticalizaiton" of medicine / health care. By severing the tie between work and medical insurance controversial expenses such as abortion, employers would no longer have to try to satisfy different constituents as to what to cover in an insurance policy. In other words, individuals according to their values and preferences would make medical expense decisions like the auto insurance television commercial asserts, "You only pay for what you need."

HSAs are currently available, and the Internal Revenue Service website[3] describes the structure and regulations.

> A Health Savings Account (HSA) is a tax-exempt trust or custodial account you set up with a qualified HSA trustee to pay or reimburse certain medical expenses you incur. You must be an eligible individual to qualify for an HSA.
>
> No permission or authorization from the IRS is necessary to establish an HSA. You set up an HSA with a trustee. A qualified HSA trustee can be a bank, an insurance company, or anyone already approved by the IRS to be a trustee

---

[3]   https://www.irs.gov/publications/p969.

of individual retirement arrangements (IRAs) or Archer MSAs. The HSA can be established through a trustee that is different from your health plan provider.

The IRS list the benefits of an HSA:

- You can claim a tax deduction for contributions you, or someone other than your employer, make to your HSA even if you don't itemize your deductions on Schedule A (Form 1040 or 1040-SR).
- Contributions to your HSA made by your employer (including contributions made through a cafeteria plan) may be excluded from your gross income.
- The contributions remain in your account until you use them.
- The interest or other earnings on the assets in the account are tax-free.
- Distributions may be tax-free if you pay qualified medical expenses.
- An HSA is "portable." It stays with you if you change employers or leave the workforce.

Under IRS guidelines, in order to qualify for an HSA, an individual must meet the following criteria:

- You are covered under a high-deductible health plan (HDHP), described later, on the first day of the month.
- You have no other health coverage except what is permitted under the guidelines.
- You aren't enrolled in Medicare.
- You can't be claimed as a dependent on someone else's 2019 tax return.

The individual and family deductibles as well as the maximum contributions to HSA for 2020 are posted on the IRS website.

	Self-only coverage	*Family coverage*
Minimum annual deductible	$1,400	$2,800
Maximum annual deductible and other out-of-pocket expenses*	$6,900	$13,800

* *This limit doesn't apply to deductibles and expenses for out-of-network services if the plan uses a network of providers. Instead, only deductibles and out-of-pocket expenses for services within the network should be used to figure whether the limit applies.*

In the single-payer system, an HSA would be a much simpler vehicle to pay for medical expenses not covered in a DPC practice or other direct payment medical practice. First, the minimum annual deductible would be eliminated, and the maximum individual annual contribution to an HSA could be $5,000 or more, which would be a tax-deductible expense, grow tax-free and would be withdrawn tax-free. A couple or family with children could deposit up to say $20,000 annually with the same tax benefits as an individual would have. An HSA would pay for such medical and health expenses such as eyeglasses, dental expenses, health and wellness activities such as personal trainers and yoga classes, long-term care insurance, etc. Individuals and families would have to become better-educated consumers and would benefit enormously as medical and health providers would have to compete vigorously for their dollars. In addition, medical and health-care providers would have to be totally transparent in their pricing, which would be posted on their websites.

The proposed HSA in a single-payer system would in effect be a super savings account for medical expenses. Individuals could deposit funds in the account as well as their employers who would get a tax deduction just as they do now for purchasing medical insurance policies for their employees. The goal is to make individuals responsible for their medical care decisions without the insurance company middlemen. Call it "patient power," "personal responsibility," "empowerment," or any other term that expresses the concept of financial independence and medical decision autonomy.

The inevitable question arises, What about low-income folks and their families? How would they fund an HSA given their low incomes? Employers would still be able to make contributions to their low-income employees' HSA accounts using current insurance payments (assuming they provide some medical insurance) and both employers and employees would be able to redirect their Medicare taxes—1.45 percent of an employee's salary—to the HSA. The HSA would become a perpetual account and therefore would be able to increase over a worker's lifetime that then can be used to pay medical expenses in retirement. Hint: this is a key proposal to begin phasing out Medicare for current workers and retirees.

One of the major criticisms of American medicine is a lack of pricing transparency. That's not the problem in Direct Primary Care and other models, where membership fees or office visits and procedures are posted prominently on the practice's website. However, transparency is a problem in general regarding medical services because patients do not currently pay for medical tests, surgery, and hospital stays. In every consumer purchase, individuals know what the seller is asking, whether they are shopping for an automobile, a house, or other item in a store or online. And consumers can always inquire about the prices charged by hair salons, automotive repair shops, dry cleaners, attorney's fees, accounting fees and other commonly purchased services, and usually have no difficulty finding the prices *online or in a newspaper advertisement. Medical care prices need to be brought into the age of technology…and transparency.*

The Surgery Center of Oklahoma posts the following on its website (Surgerycenterok.com) informing the public how the SCO is making medical care transparent and affordable.

It is no secret to anyone that the pricing of surgical services is at the top of the list of problems in our dysfunctional healthcare system. Bureaucracy at the insurance and hospital levels, cost shifting and the absence of free market principles are among the culprits for what has caused surgical care in the United States to be cost prohibitive. As more and more patients find themselves paying more and more out of pocket, it is clear that something must change. We believe that a very different approach is necessary, one involving transparent and direct pricing.

Transparent, direct, package pricing means the patient knows exactly what the cost of the service will be upfront.

Fees for the surgeon, anesthesiologist and facility are all included in one low price. There are no hidden costs, charges or surprises.

The pricing outlined on this website is not a teaser, nor is it a bait-and-switch ploy. It is the actual price you will pay. We can offer these prices because we are completely physician-owned and managed. We control every aspect of the facility from real estate costs, to the most efficient use of staff, to the elimination of wasteful operating room practices that non-profit hospitals have no incentive to curb. We are truly committed to providing the best quality care at the lowest possible price.

For a single-payer system based on individual empowerment and decision-making to succeed, all medical facilities would have to post their prices so the American people could make optimal choices regarding their medical needs. Once transparent pricing becomes more widespread, every surgical center, clinic, and hospital would fall in line to stay competitive. This is how the free market works. In a free market, prices tend to fall, as the most productive producers become the "price leaders." In the case of medical care, the Surgery Center of Oklahoma has been a pioneer in posting prices since 2009 and providing high-quality medical care for more than two decades.

MediBid.com, which is essentially the "eBay" portal for medical care, has replicated the transparency of SCO, where physicians bid for patients who want transparency, fair prices, and quality care. Medibid's customers span the gamut of self-pay/cash patients, self-funded employer groups, medical sharing groups, patients whose medical procedures not covered by insurance, and individuals seeking care via medical tourism.

MediBid's webpage (https://www.medibid.com/healthcare-auction/) explains the benefits of the auction process. The success of MediBid.com creating a free market for medicine has caught the attention of Medicare. If Medicare could utilize MediBid's portal to provide the tens of millions of beneficiaries with quality care at reasonable prices, the winners would include obviously patients and taxpayers. Physicians would benefit as well because they could reduce their overhead by eliminating most of the staff needed to fill out Medicare reimbursement claims. The next chapter will discuss how MediBid would play an integral role in putting seniors in charge of their medical care.

In the final analysis, an HSA—and MediBid—would eliminate the absurd situation where, according to Weber's *RIGGED: How Insurance Ruined Healthcare (and how to fix it)*, an MRI "can vary in price by 200 to 2000 percent." As Weber points out, Medicaid makes the lowest reimbursement rates for services, followed by Medicare, insurance companies, while "cash customers" pay the highest price for the same service physicians are willing to accept. For example, Medicaid pays $367 for an MRI and Medicare, $542, an insurance reimbursement is $695 and a cash customer would pay $1,250 but could get a discount depending how well he/she could negotiate with the hospital or clinic. Thus, as Weber explains, "The MRI clinic might lose money providing services to Medicare and Medicaid patients, and then attempts to make it up by charging more to people with insurance or who pay cash."

Weber's *RIGGED* demolishes the case for medical insurance for routine services and reveals how the insurance companies are essentially in cahoots with the medical sector to deprive consumers of real choices, free markets, transparency, and low prices.

With full transparency individuals, not insurance companies and/or providers, would "set the price" for diagnostic tests. In other words, consumers of medical care would "dictate" prices just as they do for other goods and services in a free market.

Catastrophic Insurance

Catastrophic insurance (CI) is the third component of a single-payer system. Catastrophic insurance would cover such medical expenses as open-heart surgery, complicated and extensive operations such as removing a brain tumor, or other invasive procedures and any other medical care that could not be paid from an HSA. Unlike current catastrophic insurance policies that require a high deductible, a CI in a single-payer system would not necessarily require high-deductible policy. (A high-deductible policy could be offered that would lower the annual premium, causing them to have "skin in the game.")

For example, the 150-plus million Americans now covered under employer insurance polies would be covered instead under a CI policy with virtually everyone paying $1,000 annually; the national yearly pool for catastrophic coverage would be $150-plus billion. Employers could help pay for the policy because they would no longer have to pay for traditional insurance as they do now. Any unused funds obviously would be rolled over into the following calendar year. A slightly higher premium could be charged with individuals preexisting conditions such as diabetes, obesity, and other high-risk factors, such as heart disease, etc. A regional nonprofit Catastrophic Insurance Consortium (CIC) would administer the pool. The CIC would be comprised of retired physicians and surgeons and other interested parties who would have the responsibility of working with the American people through MediBid or other portals to bring physicians and patients together at the lowest possible price for catastrophic medical care. Administrative costs therefore should be minimal, and most of the insurance premiums would go to pay for medical care.

The catastrophic insurance pool would initially be the basis for the medical care sector to adjust their prices to treat all Americans who need lifesaving procedures and operations. Instead of costs, determining prices, as is now the case in medicine, prices will determine costs. The Surgery Center of Oklahoma and MediBid.com would be the templates for the medical profession to provide the public with "fair and reasonable" prices and therefore establish a free market medical sector. For individuals who have been unhappy with the private medical insurance industry, this proposal would essentially revolutionize paying for catastrophic illnesses, which they should embrace. The CIC would be modeled after the best principles of the nonprofit sector and eliminate the unnecessary overhead of the private insurance industry.

To provide catastrophic coverage for babies in the womb and for the rest of their lives, an initial hundred-dollar annual premium would be paid into the CI pool. Once a couple knows the woman is pregnant, the premium would be paid to cover any catastrophic coverage during pregnancy and in each year in infancy. In America, 3.8 million babies are born each year, which would make the pool $380 million. So babies that are conceived in 2021 would have $100 deposited in the CI pool by their parents. The 2021 cohort would have any extraordinary medical expenses paid out of the pool, such as heart and neurological operations. And if a baby is born prematurely and needs extensive hospital care, that would be covered as a legitimate expense from the CI pool. In addition, St. Jude Hospital and the Shriners provide free care as well to youngsters who are suffering debilitating illnesses and diseases.

To ease the financial burden on couples having children the hundred-dollar premium could be a tax credit on the family's federal income tax as well as state income tax. Families and friends and neighbors could also help pay for the annual premium. The hundred-dollar annual premium would be adjusted marginally each year until the child reaches twenty-one years of age. At that time, the CIC would determine what the appropriate annual premium should be based upon the pool of funds that is in each cohort's portfolio based upon the loss ratio expected over the lifetime of that specific cohort.

Under this insurance arrangement, there would be no preexisting conditions issue because every baby would be covered from conception to end of life. This would eliminate once and for all any public debate of whether or how insurance should cover preexisting conditions. Furthermore, in keeping with free market principles, the conception to end-of-life insurance would be voluntary. If couples refuse to pay the hundred-dollar annual premium, they then take the huge risk of not getting timely and reasonably priced medical care for their child. It is hard to imagine that couples would not want to have the best medical care for their child. Thus, an extensive nationwide education campaign would have to begin so parents would realize how their family's finances would be strengthened by such a policy. In other words, a culture of personal responsibility has to be restored in America, and one way of doing it is by making parents aware of how they can provide medical care for their child and children and remove the anxiety of paying for a catastrophic illness.

Let's recap how a single-payer system based upon individual empowerment would pay for routine and other noncatastrophic medical care expenses for all Americans currently getting employer-based insurance. In addition, individuals who currently purchase expensive, high-deductible insurance policies in the open market would be able to obtain primary care, pay for other medical expenses, and be covered under catastrophic policy with the single-payer system.

The broad outline of a single-payer system has been presented above, and all the stakeholders can work out the nitty-gritty details as soon as possible.

The Medicare for All crowd would probably object to this single-payer system because there're no "guarantees." And they are 100 percent correct. There are no guarantees in life regarding the consumption of goods and services. However, the theory and practice of free markets demonstrate incontrovertibly that consumers are much better off when there is economic freedom as opposed to coercion, mandates, subsidies, and other forms of government intervention.

In short, a free market single-payer system would achieve all the goals of a government single-payer system at far lower cost and better outcomes for all the American people. And that is as close to a guarantee one could make when it comes to the free market.

Individual Single-Payer Alternative for Employer-Based Insurance

Primary care	Approximately $125 monthly, tax-deductible cost for DPC, or fee-for-service using a traditional doctor visit; estimated $300 for family of four.	Routine office visits and telemedicine and included blood tests.
Health Savings Account	Tax-deductible initial deposit up to $20,000 or more; all deposits growing tax-free and withdrawn tax-free.	Specialists, prescription drugs, medical equipment major tests, such as mammography, colonoscopy, etc., and brief hospitalizations.
Catastrophic coverage / long-term care (facility or home based)	$1,000–$4,000 tax-deductible premium per annum based on age and medical conditions.	All major operations and hospitalizations. Long-term care in a facility would be paid from this account. There should be cost sharing to avoid overuse and fraud. Deductible could be as low as $1,000 and as high as $20,000 or more for individuals and families depending on their financial risk tolerance.

Figure 2

Chapter 3

Medicare, Medicaid, and Obamacare and the Path to an Individual Single-Payer System

The greatest gap in our social security structure is the lack of adequate provision for the Nation's health...this great Nation cannot afford to allow its citizens to suffer needlessly from the lack of proper medical care.
—President Harry S. Truman, 1948 State of the Union Address

Protecting Medicaid and ensuring it remains sustainable and able to provide access to high quality care for society's most vulnerable populations is a top priority for the Trump administration.
—https://www.medicaid.gov/about-us/messages/98981

From government insurance plans with payment schedules, to medical coding, to top-down government programs waged in the name of "costs control," Washington politicians have continued to place government bureaucrats and insurance companies between a patient and their medical professional.
—Tho Bishop

I deas have consequences. And the idea that the federal government or state governments, for that matter, should pay for or subsidize the people's medical care transcends political parties, as we shall see below. Ever since Theodore Roosevelt ran for president as the Progressive party candidate in 1912, campaigning "for the passage of medical insurance that would be administered by the states," his vision for America was that "a strong country required healthy people." Who can argue with not being healthy? This begs the question of how an individual can improve his/her well-being without government plans to take care of their medical needs. But as we shall see in chapter 5, individual "wellness" is a personal responsibility, not a government task.

The election of Franklin D. Roosevelt in 1932 was a transformational event. Despite running on a fiscally conservative platform,[4] once in office, FDR did a "180." He expanded the size and scope of the federal government and changed America forever. For example, he signed the Social Security Act of 1935, which was supposed to be a modest expenditure of the federal government based upon employee-employer payroll taxes to provide some financial security for the elderly once they reach sixty-five years of age. Some of FDR's advisers wanted to include health insurance in the bill, but he vetoed that believing the country was not ready for some sort of federal government involvement in health care. Government medical care was "put on the back burner."

Nevertheless, the roots of both Medicare and Medicaid can be found in President Franklin D. Roosevelt's "Economic Bill Of Rights," which he asserted in his 1944 Annual Message to Congress on January 11. Among the so-called economic rights FDR called for, he believed we the people are entitled to "the right to adequate medical care and the opportunity to achieve and enjoy good health," as well as "the right to adequate protection from the economic fears of old age, sickness, accident, and unemployment." The passage of the Social Security program in 1935, as well as federal unemployment

---

[4] See Lawrence W. Reed's *Great Myths of the Great Depression* (https://fee.org/resources/great-myths-of-the-great-depression/).

insurance, addressed the issue of old-age economic insecurity and Great Depression unemployment. After winning reelection for an unprecedented fourth term in November 1944, FDR died a month after he was inaugurated in March 1945. VP Harry Truman succeeded FDR and wasted no time calling for more federal government intervention in medical care.

On November 19, 1945, President Truman sent a "Special Message to the Congress Recommending a Comprehensive Health Program." Two months earlier, Truman sent a message to Congress, enumerating a proposed Economic Bill of Rights, which essentially reiterated FDR's call for new "rights" supplementing the Bill of Rights.

The new president highlighted, in his message, that "the Selective Service System revealed the widespread physical and mental incapacity among the young people of our nation." According to Truman, a troubling statistic from April 1945 was that 5 million males between the ages of eighteen and thirty-seven who were unfit for military service, approximately 30 percent of the number of males who were examined for military service. Also worrisome to Truman was the fact that about 1.5 million men were discharged from the Army and Navy for physical or mental disability, which were not combat-related. Plus, an equal number of males were treated in the Armed Forces for illnesses that they had before they were inducted. Truman also pointed out that one-third of females who applied for the Women's Army Corps were rejected because they were unfit physically or mentally to serve.

Truman's conclusion regarding this situation was, in his own words, "It is more important to resolve that no American child shall come to adult life with diseases or defects which can be prevented or corrected at an early age."

Because of medical and scientific progress, people have been living longer, and many diseases, which reduced longevity decades ago, had been conquered by the mid-twentieth century. Nevertheless, Truman asserted, "The benefits of modern medical science have not been enjoyed by our citizens with any degree of equality. Nor are they today. Nor will they be in the future—*unless government is bold enough to do something about it*" (emphasis added).

Truman's collectivist vision was also on display when he asserted, "Our new Economic Bill of Rights should mean health security for all, regardless of residence, station, or race—everywhere in the United States. We should resolve now that the health of this nation is a national concern; that financial barriers in the way of attaining health shall be removed; at the health of all its citizens deserve the help of all the nation."

FDR's successor then outlined the five basic problems, which he believed the federal government should address to guarantee the health and well-being of the American people.

- Better distribution of doctors and hospitals throughout the country because of the dearth our physicians in rural communities.
- Developing public health services and maternal and childcare.
- More federal funding of medical research and better professional education.
- Addressing the high cost of individual medical care.
- Dealing with the loss of earnings when the family breadwinner is stricken with the debilitating illness.

President Truman then went into the details of each of the five problems facing the American medical sector, as he saw it, which he believed could be solved by substantial federal government intervention. He asserted, which has become the mantra of all interventionists throughout American history, "the health of American children, like education, should be recognized as a definite public responsibility." Essentially, Truman called for a universal medical care system based upon the premise that the cost of medical care should be met "through expansion of our existing compulsory social insurance system. This is not socialized medicine." In other words, Truman wanted "a system of required prepayment would not only spread the cost of medical care, it would also prevent much serious disease." Truman, therefore, conflated a compulsory federal government prepayment plan with real medical insurance. He reiterated his contention that he was not recommending socialized medicine because he claimed doctors would not be government employees; they still would be in private practice and have the ability to accept or reject patients.

To pay for his universal medical program, Truman called for a 4 percent tax on earnings up to $3,600, similar to the Social Security payroll tax, which was capped at $3,000 of wages per year. Why 4 percent? Truman pointed out that that's the percentage Americans currently were paying for medical care, and therefore, there would be no increase in their medical expenses. Low-income workers and those on public assistance would have some or all their premiums paid by the federal government and/or the states.

FDR's surgeon general, Thomas Parran, was the president's chief public voice on matters of health care. In 1946, a year after FDR passed away early in his fourth term, the surgeon general successfully helped pass the bill, which provided federal funds for hospital construction. With federal dollars of course comes strings; hospitals were legally mandated to serve all residents in their communities.

After becoming president in April 1945, Harry Truman proposed a national health insurance plan soon after taking office and again after a surprising victory in the 1948 presidential election. Although Congress did not support his national health-care bill, it did support President Truman's expansion of Social Security by providing federal funds to states to take care of the poor's medical needs, which was called Old-Age Assistance. This new entitlement laid the foundation for Medicaid twenty years later.

Today's advocates of Medicare for all have been channeling President Truman who claimed in his message seventy-four years ago, "We are a rich nation and can afford many things. But ill-health which can be prevented or cured is one thing we cannot afford."

One of the driving forces for universal medical care was Truman's desire to have a healthy pool of young men to serve in the military. In addition to being an unrepented collectivist, Truman was also a supporter of the military-industrial complex and the national security state. During President Truman's tenure in the White House, both the National Security Agency and the Central Intelligence Agency were established. Not surprisingly, Truman began to meddle overseas, a gross understatement, on the Korean Peninsula, resulting in the deaths of nearly sixty thousand American military personnel during the Korean War and the destruction of major North Korean cities. The death toll on the Korean Peninsula has been estimated to be well over two million civilians.

In short, although Truman could not get the Congress to pass his universal medical program, a portion of which was enacted twenty years later with the signing by President Johnson of both Medicare and Medicaid bills on July 30, 1965, his presidency laid the foundation for America's postwar welfare-warfare state policies, which are still with us today.

The Road to Medicare and Medicaid

In 1952, Dwight D. Eisenhower became the first Republican elected president since 1928. In some circles, there was jubilation that former general would begin to dismantle most, if not all, of FDR's New Deal. They were disappointed. In fact, Eisenhower wanted the federal government to protect insurance companies against heavy losses; Congress rejected this proposal. However, in 1956, President Eisenhower signed into law an expansion of Social Security; disability insurance now became an integral component of the federal government's involvement in health/medical care. In addition, the federal government expanded the hospital construction program by providing funds for rehabilitation facilities.

Despite rhetorically being in favor of limited government, Republicans also favored federal tax dollars for medical care. For example, Mr. Republican, conservative Senator Robert Taft of Ohio, supported federal funds to pay for the medical care of the poor that states would administer. In 1957, Representative Aime Forand of Rhode Island introduced legislation that did not pass but is considered as a model for Medicare. The Kerr-Mills bill of 1960, better known as the Medical Assistance to the Aged, was named after Senator

Kerr of Oklahoma and Representative Wilbur Mills of Arkansas, the powerful chairman of the Ways and Means Committee. This new entitlement covered the "medically needed" aged in America who did not qualify under the previously passed Old-Age Assistance program.

Although President Kennedy (1961–1963) supported national medical program for seniors, the Congress was not enthusiastic about such an expansion of the federal government into health-care matters. Kennedy supported the passage of Medicare early on in his administration, but the Senate defeated it on July 17, 1962, by a vote of 52 to 48. After JFK's assassination (November 22, 1963) and the landslide election of President Johnson, who now had Democrat majorities in both houses of Congress in 1965, Medicare and Medicaid became part of the Social Security Act, Title XVIII and Title XIX, respectively, on July 30, 1965. (We will review both programs in the next section.)

President Johnson went to Independence, Missouri—the home of former President Truman—on July 30 to sign Medicare (and Medicaid) into law. Truman and his wife, Bess, became the first two beneficiaries of the Medicare program.

Before the passage of Medicare in 1965, Senator Clinton Anderson of New Mexico, who served as President Truman's Secretary of Agriculture, was the leading sponsor of President Kennedy's Medicare bill in 1961. Meanwhile, in the House of Representatives John Byrnes (R) of Wisconsin, who served on the Ways and Means committee, proposed, in 1965, a voluntary program for retirees that would pay for physician services. This eventually became Medicare Part B and the final legislation that President Johnson signed in July 1965.

Medicare coverage took effect in 1966, which consisted of Part A, which was compulsory for all Americans sixty-five and over, and covered hospital services. A hospital trust fund was established to receive the payroll tax that was paid by both employers and employees, which at that time amounted to 0.35 percent each up to $6,600 per year, and pay for the beneficiaries' hospital bills.[5] Part B was a voluntary component of Medicare that was applied toward doctors' bills and other covered medical services. Those who enrolled in Part B paid a premium; the costs of part B were subsidized by general revenue funds.

Republican Richard Nixon sought reelection in 1972 and signed into law a sweeping expansion of Medicare. Now eligible for Social Security benefits were individuals with end-stage renal disease (ESRD). For the first time in its short history, individuals with a specific condition were entitled to Medicare funding to pay for their treatment. In addition, the Federal Supplemental Security Income program (SSI) was enacted, which provided benefits for eligible Medicaid recipients who were elderly, blind, and disabled.

President Nixon also supported federal funding to create health maintenance organizations. A key feature of the 1972 HMO Act was to provide start-up grants and loans to HMOs that met federal standards for benefits and quality. The impetus for Nixon's interventionism was to contain the rising cost of health care.

After President Nixon's resignation in August 1974, Gerald Ford succeeded him and signed the Privacy Act in order to protect personal information the federal government acquired about the American people.

When Democratic Jimmy Carter was elected in 1976, he appointed former LBJ White House aide Joseph Califano to head the Department of Health, Education, and Welfare. Califano had an ambitious agenda, namely, to prepare for a national health insurance program and to give both Medicare and Medicaid more leverage in the health-care marketplace. Working in secrecy, in March 1977, the Health Care Financing Administration was created. And with the rising cost of medical care, President Carter announced program to contain hospital costs, which failed to pass in the Congress.

After Ronald Reagan's election in 1980, the new president was immediately faced with the solvency of Social Security. The

---

[5]   A history of Medicare taxes can be found here (https://files.taxfoundation.org/legacy/docs/soc_security_rates_1937-2009-20090504.pdf).

Greenspan commission's recommendations were quickly enacted by Congress to "save" Social Security, which included raising taxes, and increasing the amount of wages that were subject to the payroll tax. Although Social Security was saved for the time being, both Medicare and Medicaid faced additional scrutiny. To address the continuing increasing costs of Medicaid, states were given more flexibility to allow recipients home and community-based services instead of being institutionalized. Waivers were also granted so states could use managed care for beneficiaries. To reduce or at least hold the line on Medicare expenditures a new payment system was instituted for inpatient hospital services, risk contracts for HMOs, and a peer review system to improve the quality of health care.

Medicare's expansion continued throughout the 1980s. Home health services were expanded and Medigap, better known as Medicare supplemental insurance, became subject to federal regulations. Hospice services were introduced in 1982

In 1986, the Secretary Bowen of HHS (Health and Human Services) supported extending Medicare to cover the cost of catastrophic illness. The Medicare Catastrophic Coverage Act of 1988 included a substantial expansion of Medicare to help the elderly pay for prescription drugs and skilled nursing facilities. To pay for the new benefits, new premiums and an income tax surcharge was levied. In 1989, HHS Secretary Louis Sullivan appointed by the newly elected George H. W. Bush discovered that upper-income seniors objected to the new benefits because many of them were receiving similar coverage from their prior employers; Congress soon repealed the new law.

New Medicare and Medicaid reforms were soon enacted in 1989. Physicians were now limited to how much extra they could charge Medicare beneficiaries above the new fee schedule. And low-income Medicare beneficiaries were assisted to pay for rising monthly premiums. In addition, Medicaid expanded benefits for pregnant women and children.

After Bill Clinton was inaugurated in 1993, he proposed the Health Security Act. The act was an attempt to provide universal health-care coverage. Congress did not pass legislation. However, in his reelection year, President Clinton signed the most comprehensive welfare reform legislation since the New Deal in August 1996. A major highlight of the bill is severing the link between Medicaid and welfare.

In the 1990s, low-income Medicare beneficiaries became eligible for Medicaid subsidizing their Part B premiums. In addition, Medicare Part C was enacted giving beneficiaries private options as well as add-on benefits, such as prescription drug coverage.

Other reforms and initiatives passed during the Clinton administration included the Health Insurance Portability and Accountability Act of 1996 (HIPAA), slowing down the rate of increase in Medicare payments, a proviso of the Balanced Budget Act of 1997, a new Medicare + Choice program to provide private health plans for beneficiaries, and the creation of State Children's Health Insurance Program (SCHIP), which extended health insurance to children whose families had incomes above the Medicaid threshold that could not afford private insurance.

George W. Bush took office in 2001 after a hotly contested presidential election. The expansion of Medicare continued into the first decade of the twenty-first century. Americans under age sixty-five with ALS, commonly referred to as Lou Gehrig's disease, were allowed to enroll in Medicare as long as they were approved for Social Security Disability Insurance (SSDI) income. In December 2003, President George W. Bush signed a major expansion of Medicare with the Prescription Drug Improvement and Modernization Act, which became known as Medicare Part D.

One of his Medicaid reforms included the Health Insurance Flexibility and Accountability waivers, which allowed states more flexibility so more low-income individuals could get health insurance coverage. In July 2001, HHS Secretary Tommy Thompson oversaw the renaming of the Health Care Financing Administration to the Centers for Medicare & Medicaid Services in order to provide more agency responsiveness to the needs of the public.

The election of Democrat Barack Obama in 2008, the first African American president, and a majority in both houses of

Congress, led to the passage of the Affordability and Accountability Act in March 2010 (a.k.a. as Obamacare). The passage of the Patient Protection and Affordable Care Act in 2010, a major leap toward creating a universal medical care system in America modeled after President Truman's vision in 1945. Obamacare will be discussed in a separate section below.

The die was cast to expand substantially the federal government's role in the medical sector and eventually pave the way for a government single-payer system.

The surprise election of Donald Trump in 2016, who ran on a promise to "repeal and replace" Obamacare, is problematic. The Supreme Court ruled Obamacare is constitutional four years earlier.[6] However, the federal tax penalty for not purchasing medical insurance was repealed in December 2017, as part of the Tax Cuts and Job Acts signed by President Trump.[7] Nevertheless, Trump still seeks to abolish Obamacare. [8]

Congress passed the Medicare and CHIP Reauthorization Act (MACRA) in 2015, whose primary goal was to pay physicians for "value and quality" medical care rather than fee-for-service reimbursement only under Medicare Part B. Medicare Part B premiums began at $3.00 per month in 1966 and now have reached $144.60 per month. However, middle- and upper-income beneficiaries have seen their premiums rise as means testing has entered the equation.

In early 2019, Medicare enrollment surpassed sixty million as the baby boom generation continues to turn sixty-five at the rate of ten thousand per day. Nearly 20 percent of the American people depend upon Medicare to pay for their medical expenses. Medicare spending is projected to be 6 percent of GDP in 2043 and 6.5 percent in 2093. However, under another set of assumptions outlined in

---

[6] https://journalofethics.ama-assn.org/article/constitutionality-affordable-care-act-update/2012-11.

[7] https://www.healthinsurance.org/obamacare-enrollment-guide/what-is-the-obamacare-penalty/.

[8] https://www.nytimes.com/2020/06/26/us/politics/obamacare-trump-administration-supreme-court.html.

the 2020 Medicare Board of Trustees annual report, Medicare spending would be 6.3 percent in 2043 in a whopping 9 percent in 2093. In short, the "graying" of America will put serious financial pressure on the federal government to fulfill its commitments to seniors over the next seven-plus decades.

But as the trustees report acknowledges, "Medicare's actual future costs are highly uncertain for reasons apart from the inherent challenges in projecting healthcare cost growth over time." This is another example of a top-down federal spending program, which also can be described as "trickle-down economics," in the sense that tax dollars flow—more accurately expropriated from taxpayers—to Washington and then those funds "trickle down" to doctors, hospitals, pharmaceutical companies, medical equipment manufacturers, and all the other participants in the delivery of medical services.

To help shore up Medicare Part multibillionaire senior citizens like Warren Buffett, Michael Bloomberg, and others like multimillionaires Bill and Hillary Clinton should not have their Medicare Part A subsidized by low- and middle-income workers. If billionaires and multimillionaires want to help out their fellow citizens, instead of calling for a wealth tax, they should propose paying their own way for Medicare benefits. That seems to be the only fair way to eliminate subsidies for individuals who certainly have the means to pay for their own federal government mandated medical programs.

The trustees conclude in this section of the report "that Congress and the executive branch work closely together with a sense of urgency to address these challenges."

Medicaid and the Challenges It Faces in the Twenty-First Century

On July 30, 1965, President Johnson signed legislation that created both Medicare and Medicaid. Medicaid is a joint federal government-state government program that covers low-income individuals and families who meet strict eligibility requirements and is available in all states, the District of Columbia and US territories. Although the federal government created Medicaid, each state has flexibility under federal guidelines to administer the program. In 2018, total federal and state Medicaid spending was $597.4 billion, or 9.5 percent of federal spending, making it the third largest domestic program in the federal budget.

As of April 2019, more than 72 million Americans were enrolled in Medicaid and the Children's Health Insurance Program (CHIP). Nearly 66 million individuals were enrolled in Medicaid and 6.6 million were enrolled and CHIP. In addition, Medicaid is the principal provider in terms of funding for the long-term care of Americans in nursing homes and provides a substantial flow of federal taxpayer dollars for hospitals, community health centers, physicians, nursing homes, and jobs in the medical sector.

To put this all in perspective, Medicaid provides insurance coverage for one in five Americans, assistance to ten million Medicare beneficiaries and provides more than 50 percent of long-term care financing in the country. Moreover, Medicaid spends nearly 17 percent of every dollar devoted to medical care in the United States. The primary driver of Medicare costs is the elderly and persons with disabilities who consume nearly two-third of all Medicaid spending even though this cohort represents 25 percent of enrollees while children 43 percent of all Medicaid beneficiaries.

Medicaid's "safety net" pays for approximately half of all births in most states, more than 80 percent of poor children, nearly 50 percent of children with special medical needs, and 45 percent of the nonelderly population with such disabilities as autism, traumatic brain injury, mental illness, and Alzheimer's disease. And in some states, Medicaid provides assistance for higher-income families with children who have significant disabilities.

A comprehensive itemization of Medicaid expenditures is beyond the scope of this book. A detailed analysis of Medicaid's funding and expenditures as available at the Henry J. Kaiser Family

Foundation (KFF.org), which is a nonprofit organization, based in San Francisco California.[9]

Nevertheless, the issue brief, "10 Things to Know About Medicaid: Setting the Facts Straight," published in March 2019, makes several assertions in its conclusion, all of which amount to a ringing endorsement of Medicaid, both the means (taxpayer dollars) and ends—providing medical care for tens of millions of Americans of Medicaid. The brief cites public opinion polls that reveal widespread public support for Medicaid across the political spectrum. A more cogent explanation of the polling results is that the world first-aid ideology is deeply embedded in the American people's psyche. This is not surprising given the decades of propaganda from the political class, intellectuals, and others who have been cheerleaders for big government solutions to social issues.

The brief concludes with the following statement: "Congress and states could also consider broader health reform that could expand the role of public programs in health care including Medicare for All or Medicaid buy-in programs that could have significant implications for Medicaid."

Although the Henry J. Kaiser Family Foundation is a "nonpartisan" organization, it is certainly in the ideological camp of supporting big government solutions to providing medical care to tens of millions of Americans.

However, there are alternatives to Medicaid, which we will explore in chapter 4—the nonprofit solution that is based upon quintessential American values—voluntarism and mutual aid.

---

[9] See "Medicaid Financing: The Basics" (https://www.kff.org/medicaid/issue-brief/medicaid-financing-the-basics/); "10 Things to Know About Medicaid: Setting the Facts Straight" (https://www.kff.org/medicaid/issue-brief/10-things-to-know-about-medicaid-setting-the-facts-straight/); and the Medicaid website (https://www.medicaid.gov).

The Affordable Care Act (ACA) and Its Impact on the Medical Care Sector

On March 23, 2010, President Obama signed the Affordable Care Act (ACA), which is generally referred to Obamacare. The major goal of Obamacare was to reduce the number of uninsured Americans. In 2013, more than forty-four million nonelderly Americans did not have health insurance. When the ACA went into effect, in 2014, more nonelderly adults were able to obtain Medicaid coverage, and others who qualified took advantage of tax credits by purchasing coverage through a health insurance marketplace. By 2016, the number of uninsured dropped to just under twenty-seven million. [10]

Other significant provisions of the ACA included young adults being able to remain on their parents private plans until age twenty-six as per a new mandate. Insurers are prevented from denying coverage to anyone with a preexisting condition and charging them a higher premium. However, within limits, older adults may be charged more for coverage. A requirement that virtually *all* Americans purchase health insurance or be subject to a tax penalty was a controversial component the ACA. The goal was to make sure that insurance companies would have healthy as well as unhealthy new beneficiaries to prevent adverse selection in the insurance industry. (The tax penalty effectively disappeared in 2019 because the Trump administration reduced the penalty to zero dollars as a way of decreasing the burden of the ACA*.)

The decline in the number of uninsured Americans is considered by proponents of Obamacare as one of its important achievements. However, in 2017, the number of uninsured rose by more than half a million. This is attributed to the fact that some states did not increase the Medicaid expansion for low-income individuals

---

[10] For a comprehensive review of the ACA see "The Uninsured and the ACA: A Primer—Key Facts about Health Insurance and the Uninsured amidst Changes to the Affordable Care Act," https://www.kff.org/report-section/the-uninsured-and-the-aca-a-primer-key-facts-about-health-insurance-and-the-uninsured-amidst-changes-to-the-affordable-care-act-introduction/.

and families. Nevertheless, slightly more than half of the remaining uninsured are eligible for ACA assistance while the other half are ineligible because of their immigration status or live in a state where Medicaid has not been expanded.

The ACA mandates included penalties for employers (firms with fifty or more full-time equivalent employees) who did not offer employees affordable coverage. Employers who offered policies covering 60 percent or more of medical expenses could avoid any penalties.

According to the executive summary of *The Uninsured and the ACA: A Primer,*

> Health insurance makes a difference in whether and when people get necessary medical care, where they get their care, and ultimately, how healthy they are. Uninsured people are far more likely than those with insurance to postpone healthcare or forgo it altogether. The consequences can be severe, particularly when preventable conditions or chronic diseases go undetected. *While the safety net of public hospitals, community clinics and health centers, and local providers provides a crucial healthcare source for uninsured people, it does not close the access for the uninsured.* (Emphasis added*)*

This statement succinctly captures the essence of not only Obamacare but government intervention in medical insurance— incorrectly termed health insurance—that goes to the heart of the issue, namely, why does the federal government or the states have any role whatsoever in paying, which requires substantial taxes, for Medicare, Medicaid, and the ACA?

This is the question we will tackle next. How can everyone, no matter what their income is or health status, have access to medical care? President Truman envisioned the current top-down approach in 1945, and his goal of national "health care" began to be a reality by Presidents Johnson in 1965, Bush in 2003, and Obama in 2010. Thus, the initial intervention and expansion of the federal government's mandates, subsidies, grants, and other forms of taxpayer dollars to provide "health" benefits to the American people—primarily low-income children, poor adults, and senior citizens no matter their income and net worth—has put us on the road to eventually reach Medicare to All.

In other words, the federal government has cast a wide social safety net that includes virtually every constituency in America, thereby making both Medicare and Medicaid popular among the citizenry across the political spectrum. According to October 2018 poll, 53 percent of the American people had a favorable view of Obamacare. By June 2019, the ACA had a 46 percent favorable approval rating.

Thus, as long as more government intervention in medical care becomes a more acceptable "mainstream" idea and as Medicare for All is being touted as a credible proposal to provide medical care for 330 million Americans, the propaganda for a government single-payer system will intensify. We cannot rule out, therefore, a total government takeover of medical care if a single-payer system becomes more appealing to young adults, families with children who have substantial medical needs and seniors who want to have more "freebies" to deal with chronic conditions in their golden years.

Empowering Medicare and Medicaid Beneficiaries

Medicare is "big business." How big a business? In 2019, Medicare spent nearly $800 billion for the 61.2 million beneficiaries, which included 52.6 million aged sixty-five and older Americans and 8.7 million disabled Americans. Figure 3 outlines Medicare's breakdown of income and expenditures. The data was compiled for the 2020 Medicare Trustees report—the annual report submitted to the Congress on the status of the medical program for the Nation's seniors and its future prospects.[11]

Medicare's income is primarily generated from payroll taxes, $285.1 billion, general revenue, $268.2 billion, and premiums, $99.4 billion. As far as expenditures go the major outlays included hospitals, $206.9 billion and Medicare Part C, also known as Medicare Advantage, the option that nearly 40 percent of Medicare beneficiaries use to get their coverage from private health plans, cost $273.8 billion. And finally, the prescription drug benefit cost $97.1 billion. When all the Medicare expenditures are added up, the average benefit per enrollee totaled nearly $14,000.

Table II.B1.—Medicare Data for Calendar Year 2019

	HI or Part A	SMI Part B	SMI Part D	Total
Assets at end of 2018 (billions)	$200.4	$96.3	$8.0	$304.7
Total income	$322.5	$373.6	$98.7	$794.8
Payroll taxes	285.1	—	—	285.1
Interest	6.5	2.6	0.1	9.1
Taxation of benefits	23.8	—	—	23.8
Premiums	3.9	99.4	15.8	119.1
General revenue	1.3	268.2	70.2	339.8
Transfers from States	—	—	12.3	12.3
Other	1.8	3.4	0.4	5.6
Total expenditures	$328.3	$370.3	$97.6	$796.2
Benefits	322.8	365.7	97.1	785.6
Hospital	147.3	59.6	—	206.9
Skilled nursing facility	27.6	—	—	27.6
Home health care	7.0	11.4	—	18.4
Physician fee schedule services	—	74.2	—	74.2
Private health plans (Part C)	119.1	154.7	—	273.8
Prescription drugs	—	—	97.1	97.1
Other	21.9	65.8	—	87.7
Administrative expenses	5.5	4.6	0.5	10.6
Net change in assets	−$5.8	$3.3	$1.2	−$1.4
Assets at end of 2019	$194.6	$99.6	$9.2	$303.3
Enrollment (millions)				
Aged	52.2	48.2	40.2	52.6
Disabled	8.7	7.9	7.0	8.7
Total	60.9	56.1	47.2	61.2
Average benefit per enrollee	$5,305	$6,517	$2,057	$13,879

Note: Totals do not necessarily equal the sums of rounded components.

Figure 3

---

[11] https://www.cms.gov/files/document/2020-medicare-trustees-report.pdf, page 10.

A further breakdown of Medicare's income reveals that Part A or HI, which pays for hospital expenses, is funded primarily from payroll taxes. The payroll tax of 1.45 percent is levied on both employers and employees, with no income cap; self-employed workers pay 2.9 percent of their net earnings. Since 2013, high-income workers have paid an additional 0.9 percent tax. The tax kicks in at $200,000 for single taxpayers and $250,000 for married couples. In other words, Medicare beneficiaries do not directly pay for their hospital insurance benefits, which instead are paid by current workers.

During their working careers, Medicare beneficiaries had paid the payroll tax, which was used to pay for the benefits of retirees. In short, funding for Part A is in effect an intergenerational chain letter, more aptly called a Ponzi scheme. Of course, it is very politically incorrect to describe the funding of Medicare Part A as such, but that is the reality that policymakers dare not address regarding this shaky funding scheme because it would upset the tens of millions of Medicare beneficiaries.

Beneficiaries pay a $1,408 deductible for each Part A benefit period and then coinsurance for hospital stays outlined in the Medicare Cost Schedule.

Medicare Part B's income primarily comes from general revenue ($268.2 billion) and premiums ($99.4 billion). Taxpayers, who foot the bill for one of the welfare states most popular programs, therefore heavily subsidize Medicare beneficiaries. The prescription drug benefit, Part D, a $97 billion expenditure, receives a huge subsidy as well, $70.2 billion from taxpayers. Premiums, in effect out-of-pocket expenses for beneficiaries, were less than $16 billion, in 2019. Also, after beneficiaries pay a $198 deductible for Part B, they "typically pay 20% of the Medicare-approved amount for most doctor services [including most doctor services while you're a hospital inpatient], outpatient therapy, and durable medical equipment [DME]."

Given all the out-of-pocket costs associated with Parts A and B, what is the average "gap" coverage that beneficiaries pay to cover the 20 percent that Medicare does not pay for Part B? According to Medicare's website, monthly premiums range from a high-deduct plan, Medigap Plan G, $47–$74 per month to a high for Medigap

Plan C, $329, for residents of Bergen County, New Jersey. Rates vary by geographic area and can be determined on this page: https://www. medicare.gov/medigap-supplemental-insurance-plans/. Retirees in different counties could obtain quotes by accessing this page when they search for an appropriate plan.

A quick overview of Medicare Part B premiums is pertinent in terms of replacing Medicare with a single-payer system without taxpayer subsidies. Currently, beneficiaries who earn $87,000 or less and file and individual tax return pay the standard monthly premium of $144.60. Couples who file a joint tax return earning $174,000 pay the same premium.

The following table[12] from Medicare highlights the higher Part B premiums beneficiaries have to pay. In other words, Part B has been "means tested." The premium is based on taxpayers' income two years prior to receiving benefits. This is called the income-related monthly adjusted amount, IRMAA.

For 2020, the premium was assessed based on income received in 2018 when beneficiaries may still have been working and earning a higher income. Thus, Medicare uses data, which penalizes some beneficiaries for being a high-income earner when they first enroll in Medicare Part B. In retirement, as their income tends to decline, their premium would decline as well.

The substantial subsidies that Medicare beneficiaries receive are the primary reason it is probably the most popular government program. Very few Medicare beneficiaries could afford to pay the nearly $14,000 cost per enrollee. This is how the welfare state operates— provide benefits to a huge voting bloc, which is a reliable interest group to perpetuate the redistribution of income policies, in this case from working people to retirees, some of whom are wealthy and could afford to pay for all their medical needs on their own.

---

[12] https://www.medicare.gov/Pubs/pdf/11579-Medicare-Costs.pdf.

If your yearly income in 2018 was			You pay (in 2020)
File individual tax return	File joint tax return	File married and separate tax return	
$87,000 or less	$174,000 or less	$87,000 or less	$144.60
above $87,000 up to $109,000	above $174,000 up to $218,000	not applicable	$202.40
above $109,000 up to $136,000	above $218,000 up to $272,000	not applicable	$289.20
above $136,000 up to $163,000	above $272,000 up to $326,000	not applicable	$376.00
above $163,000 and less than $500,000	above $326,000 and less than $750,000	above $87,000 and less than $413,000	$462.70
$500,000 or above	$750,000 and above	$413,000 and above	$491.60

Figure 4

In a similar vein, the monthly premium for Part D, the prescription drug benefit, is based upon a sliding scale as well.[13]

---

13 https://www.medicare.gov/Pubs/pdf/11579-Medicare-Costs.pdf.

If your yearly income in 2018 was			You pay (in 2020)
File individual tax return	File joint tax return	File married and separate tax return	
$87,000 or less	$174,000 or less	$87,000 or less	Your plan premium
above $87,000 up to $109,000	above $174,000 up to $218,000	not applicable	$12.20 + your plan premium
above $109,000 up to $136,000	above $218,000 up to $272,000	not applicable	$31.50 + your plan premium
above $136,000 up to $163,000	above $272,000 up to $326,000	not applicable	$50.70 + your plan premium
above $163,000 and less than $500,000	above $326,000 and less than $750,000	above $87,000 and less than $413,000	$70.00 + your plan premium
$500,000 or above	$750,000 and above	$413,000 and above	$76.40 + your plan premium

Figure 5

Medicare's $796 billion budget was funded by $339.8 billion from general revenue, $285.1 billion in payroll taxes, $119.1 billion in premiums, and $23.8 billion of income from taxation of benefits. With the huge subsidy of nearly $340 billion, how can Medicare beneficiaries pay for all their expenses given that tens of millions of retirees have relatively low incomes? In addition, Medicare beneficiaries are used to getting their expenses paid by a government-created agency for more than fifty years. However, Medicare Part C, where expenses are paid through private insurance companies, seems like a "market-based" solution but in reality is another example of "too much" insurance used to pay for routine medical expenses.

Medicare parts B and D are partially funded by premiums outlined in figures 4 and 5. These premiums could be used to pay for routine doctors' visits via a Direct Primary Care practice or similar method described in chapter 2, as well as fund an HSA to pay for specialist visits and diagnostic tests.

For example, if the average monthly fee of a DPC membership is $125, or $1,500 annually, or $3,000 for a couple, Medicare beneficiaries would be able to replace the need for some of part B or Part C's expenses. In addition, all current Medicare beneficiaries could create an HSA and deposit some of their current savings, an IRA or 401(k), and use some of their income to take greater control of their medical expenses. The monies placed in a senior citizen HSA would be tax-deductible, grow tax-free, and taken out of the account tax-free. In addition, any funds used to pay for a DPC membership would also be tax-deductible beyond the standard deduction, which most taxpayers now pay.

The transition to an individual single-payer system empowering senior citizens must provide immediate benefits such as tax deductibility, which would allow them to fund their own accounts in order to pay for routine and specialized medical care as well as prescription drugs.[14]

To replace Part A, which covers hospital expenses, Medicare beneficiaries would pay for such coverage from an HSA and/or catastrophic policy / long-term care policy. Currently, Part A expenditures of $328.3 billion would be reduced using proven techniques to lower medical care costs in the country such as greater competition via MediBid.com, telemedicine, etc.

If we assume that there is at least 20 percent to 30 percent "waste, fraud, and abuse" in all medical expenses, then expenditures for retirees and the disabled could be reduced by as much as $240 billion, not including the out-of-pocket expenses as deductibles, co-pays, and other fees, which add to the total unnecessary spending. No matter what the actual overspending is for retirees, the current

---

[14] Medicare's coverage is outlined here, https://www.medicare.gov/your-medicare-costs/medicare-costs-at-a-glance.

out-of-pocket expenses plus the tax-deductibility contributions to individual accounts to fund the three pillars of a single-payer system—direct primary care, an HSA, and a catastrophic/long-term care policy—should provide the resources to allow current Medicare beneficiaries to pay for their medical care on their own.

For example, to lower the costs of major operations, hip and knee replacement, back surgery, heart valve repair, and other cardiac procedures, MediBid.com would be a fundamental component of consumer-driven prices. Physicians from around the country and indeed the world would bid for individuals' business. As uncomfortable as this may seem—and unseemly—to some (many), the evidence is overwhelming that patients obtain high-quality medical care through MediBid.com, where testimonials and videos explaining how the bidding process substantially lowers medical costs.

To recap, current Medicare beneficiaries can take charge of their medical care under an individual single-payer system that would be funded with their own funds. A breakdown of the costs would be as follows:

Individual Single-Payer Alternative for Medicare Beneficiaries

Primary care	Approximately $125 monthly, tax-deductible cost for DPC, or fee-for-service using a traditional doctor visit.	Routine office visits and telemedicine and included blood tests.
Health savings account	Tax-deductible initial deposit up to $20,000 or more; all deposits growing tax-free and withdrawn tax-free.	Specialists, prescription drugs, medical equipment major tests, such as mammography, colonoscopy, etc., and brief hospitalizations.

Catastrophic coverage / long-term care (facility or home based)	$2,000–$4,000 tax-deductible premium per annum.	All major operations and hospitalizations. Long-term care in a facility would be paid from this account. There should be cost sharing to avoid overuse and fraud. Deductible to be determined by Catastrophic Insurance Consortium.

Figure 6

There would be no co-pays, deductibles for virtually most medical expenses, because each service would be paid "out of pocket" or by the Catastrophic Insurance Consortium, which could be the major insurance companies unlike the nonprofit one cited in chapter 2.

Would Medicare beneficiaries be better off under a new single-payer system instead of the current single-payer system and Medigap coverage, and would there be universal coverage of seniors given the substantial number current beneficiaries who have low incomes?

As a transition to single-payer system, both low-income and disabled beneficiaries could get their catastrophic coverage covered say for three to five years or more with general revenue that is currently used to pay for Parts B and D. During the transition period, individuals and couples would have to save so they would eventually have to pay some portion of the catastrophic coverage, and nonprofit health organizations would also kick in to pay the annual premiums.

But the greatest contribution to catastrophic coverage would come from hospitals, which would create a special fund for low-income Medicare recipients, who would get major operations and other benefits from this pool of money. Tax-deductible contributions, but preferably tax credits, would be the incentive for members of the community to increase support for hospitals. The next chapter will describe how the nonprofit sector would provide assistance to low-income Americans.

Medicaid: The Transition to a Single-Payer System

President Johnson signed Medicaid—and Medicare—into law on the same day in 1965 as former president Harry Truman looked on with his wife, Bess. In just two short decades, the unthinkable happened in America: medical care for the elderly and low-income Americans became a government responsibility. In addition, the federal government foisted a financial burden on states, which had to obey the dictates of Uncle Sam to provide medical care for low-income citizens. This put another nail in the coffin of federalism—the principle that the federal government had certain responsibilities as outlined in the Constitution and states would be "laboratories of democracy" to decide for themselves what policies to enact that would be in the best interest of their citizens. With the passage of Medicaid, state spending on medical care would be determined, to a large degree, by the federal government.

From its modest beginnings more than four decades ago in 2018, Medicaid spent $597.4 billion, which provided benefits for 64 million individuals and 6.8 million children under the Children's Health Insurance Program (CHIP), which was enacted into law in 1997 to provide "federal matching funds to states to provide health coverage to children in families with incomes too high to qualify for Medicaid, but who can't afford private coverage."

One obvious conclusion about Medicaid is that nearly 25 percent of the American people are dependent upon the government for medical care. In other words, one out of four Americans don't have the financial resources to take care of themselves when it comes to a doctor's visit, prescription drugs, diagnostic testing, or hospital stay after an operation. Nevertheless, analysts have praised Medicaid and its expansion under Obamacare as a boon to low-income individuals and families.[15] On the other side of the issue is Sally Pipes, president of the Pacific Research Institute, who has several critical essays citing research about the poor outcomes of Medicaid recipients in her *Forbes* columns (https://www.forbes.com/sites/sallypipes/#3d8a13a1541b), as well on her organization's website (https://www.pacificresearch. org/team/sally-c-pipes/).

This section will not review the merits of Medicaid except to point out that the American people are overinsured in yet another attempt to provide medical care to large segments of the population by using traditional medical insurance. Furthermore, phasing out Medicaid would relieve taxpayers of the more than $600 billion (estimated 2020 outlays) extracted from them by force to pay for other people's medical needs. And if it can show there would be better outcomes and universal coverage for all Medicaid and CHIP recipients under the individual single-payer system—in other words, no one would be left behind regarding access to medical care—the current high support for Medicaid across the political spectrum would evaporate.

Obtaining medical care should not be more complicated than getting any service we currently consume—cable TV, cell phone, health and beauty care, and other services we pay for out of pocket. When it comes to medical care, however, the conventional thinking is that somehow we need "insurance" in order to pay for routine office visits, prescription drugs, and diagnostic tests when the rational use of insurance is only for catastrophic losses. Instead, the American people have been used to getting their medical needs paid by an insurance company, which in turn gets paid by the employer and more often than not with employees chipping in for the (high) premiums and the federal and state governments, which pay for Medicare and Medicaid and subsidize individuals relying on the state exchanges under Obamacare.

---

[15] See Hannah, Katch, Jesse Cross-Call, and Matt Broaddus's "Frequently Asked Questions About Medicaid," Center for Budget and Policy Priorities, November 22, 2019, https://www.cbpp.org/research/correcting-seven-myths-about-medicaid.

Shouldn't low-income individuals and families have access to quality medical care without having to go through a bureaucratic maze that can be found at Medicaid.gov? The page below highlights the pages where all the rules, regulations, mandates and arbitrary guidelines the federal government has enacted in order for Medicaid recipients to receive benefits. As a nation, we can do better. The individual single-payer system that already has been outlined for employees who receive employer-based insurance and Medicare beneficiaries can now be applied to Medicaid recipients.

Medicaid State Plan Amendments

Indian Health & Medicaid
History
Indian Health Care Improvement Act
American Recovery & Reinvestment Act
Tribal Affairs Guidance & Resources

Home & Community Based Services
Home & Community Based Services Authorities
HCBS Training
Guidance
Statewide Transition Plans
Technical Assistance

Eligibility
Estate Recovery
MAGI Conversion Plan
Seniors & Medicare and Medicaid Enrollees
Verification Plans
Minimum Essential Coverage
Spousal Impoverishment
Medicaid Third Party Liability & Coordination of Benefits
Medicaid Eligibility Quality Control

Prescription Drugs
Branded Prescription Drug Fee Program
Covered Outpatient Drugs Policy
Drug Utilization Review
Excluded Drug Coverage
Federal Upper Limits
HCV Communication
Medicaid Drug Rebate Program
Pharmacy Pricing
Program Releases
State Drug Utilization Data
State Prescription Drug Resources
Retail Price Survey

Access to Care
Access Monitoring Review Plans

Outreach Tools
Supporting Enrollment Efforts
Helping Connect Enrollees to Care
Living Well

Program Information
Medicaid & CHIP Eligibility Levels
Medicaid & CHIP Enrollment Data
Medicaid & CHIP Marketplace Interactions
Targeted Enrollment Strategies
Eligibility Verification Policies

Financial Management
Payment Limit Demonstrations
Disproportionate Share Hospitals
Medicaid Administrative Claiming
State Expenditure Reporting for Medicaid & CHIP
Provider Preventable Conditions
Actuarial Report on the Financial Outlook for Medicaid
Section 223 Demonstration Program to Improve Community Mental Health Services

Long Term Services & Supports
Health Homes
Balancing Incentive Program
Integrating Care
Community Living
Employment Initiatives
Institutional Long Term Care
Money Follows the Person
PACE
Alternatives to Psychiatric Residential Treatment Facilities Demonstration
Real Choice Systems Change
Reports & Evaluations
Self-Directed Services
TEFT Program
Workforce Initiative

Program Integrity
National Correct Coding Initiative
Affordable Care Act Program Integrity Provisions

Quality of Care
Medicaid Managed Care
Performance Measurement
Improvement Initiatives
Releases & Announcements

Section 1115 Demonstrations
About 1115 Demonstrations
How States Apply
Transparency
1115 Demonstration Monitoring & Evaluation
1115 Community Engagement Initiative
State Waivers List
1115 Substance Use Disorder Demonstrations
Coronavirus Disease 2019 (COVID-19): Section 1115 Demonstrations

Data & Systems
Medicaid Enterprise Systems Newsletter
MACBIS
Medicaid Information Technology Architecture
Medicaid Management Information System
Medicaid Enterprise Certification Toolkit
Medicaid Eligibility & Enrollment Toolkit
Medicaid Enterprise Reuse
Health Information Technology/
Health Information Exchange
IT Procurement Opportunities
Outcomes-Based Certification

Cost Sharing
Cost Sharing Exemptions
Out of Pocket Costs

Enrollment Strategies
Continuous Eligibility
Express Lane Eligibility
Lawfully Residing Immigrant Children & Pregnant Women
Presumptive Eligibility

Managed Care
Managed Care Authorities
Enrollment Report
Managed Care Entities
Guidance
Managed LTSS
Profiles & Program Features
Technical Assistance

Benefits
Alternative Benefit Plans
Autism Services
Behavioral Health Services
Dental Care
Early and Periodic Screening, Diagnostic, and Treatment
Hospice Benefits
Mandatory & Optional Medicaid Benefits
Prevention
Telemedicine

Figure 7

126

Under the individual single-payer (ISP) system, Medicaid recipients would obtain primary care from one of many venues. The medical "infrastructure" is already in place for Medicaid recipients.

First, routine medical care would be available from community nonprofit health centers, which would screen the income of patients as per their guidelines in order to avoid free riders. The income cut off would vary from rural communities to relatively high-income urban and suburban areas. The nonprofits could provide office visits for free and request donations from patients or require a small charge, let's say $5 to $10 or more per visit. Or the nonprofit could in effect model its services after a Direct Primary Care practice and charge a low monthly fee or the individual or family. This will provide a steady cash flow to nonprofits, reducing their need for fundraising.

Millions of very low-income families could easily obtain their routine medical care from nonprofit centers. The number of centers would have to scale up substantially in order to meet the needs of this demographic in the years ahead. Retired physicians would be the potential pool of doctors to staff these facilities. In addition, physicians who donate their time to a nonprofit could receive a tax credit for their pro bono work. For example, a physician who donates his/her time and treats fifty patients per year could receive a tax credit, let's say of $50 per patient, which would be deductible from both federal and state income taxes. In states where there is no income tax, the federal tax credit could be increased, let's say to $75.

Second, Walmart, CVS, Walgreens already have clinics, and their respective stores offer low prices for office visits and other routine care for low-income individuals and families who easily could afford the fees charged by these clinics.

The transition, therefore, for Medicaid recipients to receive primary care in an ISP system would be relatively seamless and take place over several years. The federal government would announce that beginning in 2022 Medicaid recipients would receive their primary care outlined in figure 8 based upon the discussion above. To hasten the transition, Medicaid recipients could receive a stipend of $500 in early 2021. Those funds would be used to pay for primary care in that year, giving recipients the opportunity to "shop around" the best care in their communities. Any funds not used in 2021 could be placed in a health savings account for future expenditures and earning tax-free interest.

The next major challenge is to provide Medicaid recipients with catastrophic coverage. The best way to achieve this goal is for hospitals to create a fund for charitable donations to pay for the care of low-income individuals and families. Again, individuals who make these contributions would receive federal and/or state income tax credits. Tax credits would provide a huge incentive for members of every community in the country to replace Medicaid hospital care and major catastrophic expenses with charitable donations. This would be a win-win for everyone in the country. Medicaid recipients will have access to the top hospitals in their communities with the best surgeons and doctors, taxpayers would no longer be forced to pay for Medicaid, and hospitals would have to become superefficient in order to attract donors who would want their charitable contributions to be used wisely and effectively.

The real losers in this proposal would be, of course, the bureaucrats overseeing Medicaid and all the federal and state workers who have to administer the program. However, individuals are not placed on earth to feed any government bureaucracy. Human beings have an important role in society—that is to provide needed goods and services to their fellow human beings in a peaceful manner. This is one of the important lessons of economics and the foundation of how to create a free, just, and peaceful society.

Individual Single-Payer Alternative for Medicaid Recipients

Primary care	Nonprofit medical centers based on Volunteers in Medicine model; pro bono physician services; big box stores medical centers.	Routine office visits and telemedicine and included blood tests
Health Savings Account	Contributions by foundations, individuals, etc. to fund accounts; nonprofit medical centers to provide care, if possible; specialists can provide services pro bono, for which they would receive a tax credit, or for a small charge.	Specialists, prescription drugs, medical equipment major tests, such as mammography, colonoscopy, etc., and brief hospitalizations
Catastrophic coverage / long-term care (facility or home based)	Hospitals to provide charity care funded by tax-deductible (tax credits) donations.	All major operations and hospitalizations. Long-term care in a facility would be paid from this account. There should be cost sharing to avoid overuse and fraud.

Figure 8

What will be the cost of medical care for current Medicaid recipients in our proposed ISP system? The short answer is a lot lower than it is today. Why? Several reasons. First, there would be no federal and state bureaucracies administering Medicaid. There would be less need for administrative staff in physicians' offices to file Medicaid claims. Second, there will be more competition among physicians and hospitals for medical care dollars. And competition invariably lowers prices. Third, the American people overwhelmingly support Medicaid, presumably because they want to help their fellow citizens who do not have the resources to pay their "own way" when it comes to medical care. However, if the American people could be shown how they can continue to embrace a "culture of caring" with their charitable contributions, which would increase support for nonprofit medical centers and hospitals, and provide current Medicaid recipients with better medical care, why would they object?

In other words, to phase out Medicaid as quickly as possible, the American people would have to "pony up the money." The major objection to replacing Medicare with and ISP is ideological, namely, as we have shown, there is a visceral opposition to free market (i.e., voluntary) medicine as it relates to helping low-income families because there are no "guarantees" that the people will step up to the plate and provide enough of their own money voluntarily to support the nonprofit health sector. This is a bogus criticism.

The premise that government coercion—taxes—to achieve a social "good"—helping families get medical care—is legitimate is a dubious assertion, to say the least. It is no different from the Chinese government restricting couples from having more than one child. The framework for a noncoercive, compassionate, high-quality alternative to Medicaid has been outlined. It would be up to the American people to return to our philosophical and practical roots—nonprofitization.

Replacing Obamacare

On the tenth anniversary of the passage of the Affordable Care Act, popularly known as Obamacare,[16] the *New York Times* had an

---

[16] For an overview of Obamacare, see https://www.ehealthinsurance.com/resources/affordable-care-act/history-timeline-affordable-care-act-aca.

extensive article ("Obamacare Turns 10: A Look at What Works And What Doesn't," March 24)[17] reflecting on the programs successes and shortcomings.

Prior to the passage of Obama care 22.3 percent of adult between the ages of eighteen and sixty-four were uninsured; by 2016, that number had declined to 12.4 percent. Obamacare increased the number of insured by twenty million.

Although the original legislation required states to expand Medicaid in 2012, the Supreme Court ruled that states could not be compelled to do so. Nevertheless, states that expanded Medicaid under the ACA has been reflected in the fact that thirteen million more Americans have enrolled in Medicaid. In addition, the ACA outlawed limits on lifetime or annual caps by insurance companies and also required insurers to cover children beneficiaries until the age of twenty-six.

One of the more controversial components of Obamacare was the tax penalty for not purchasing insurance. According to Healthcare.gov.,

> For plan years through 2018, if you can afford health insurance but choose not to buy it, you may pay a fee called the individual Shared Responsibility Payment when you file your **federal taxes**. (The fee is sometimes called the "penalty," "fine," or "individual mandate.")
>
> Starting with the 2019 plan year (for which you'll file taxes by July 15, 2020), the Shared Responsibility Payment no longer applies.
>
> **Note:** Some states have their own individual health insurance mandate, requiring you to have qualifying health coverage or pay a fee with your **state taxes** for the 2019 plan year. If you live in

---

[17] https://www.nytimes.com/2020/03/23/health/obamacare-aca-coverage-cost-history.html.

a state that requires you to have health coverage
and you don't have coverage (or an exemption).

The mandate was removed in the 2017 tax-cut bill that President Trump signed in December of that year.

One of the major criticisms of Obamacare according to the *New York Times* article, "For many Americans, the 'Affordable' part of the Affordable Care Act has seemed like an empty promise, as premiums, deductibles and other out-of-pocket costs continue to be an extraordinary burden on millions of households."

However, one example in the article about Obamacare's benefits makes this point: "But the law has made health care far more affordable in a number of less conspicuous ways. That has allowed Erik Westlund and Dr. Christina Cifra, of Iowa City, to afford their 4-year-old son's care. He has hemophilia and needs a clotting factor that costs roughly $26,000 a month, or $312,000 a year. They are insured, through Dr. Cifra's job but his more than $1.2 million in medical bills to date would have easily surpassed many employers' lifetime caps before the ACA."

No doubt there are many, many examples of how expensive medical care has been covered under the Affordable Care Act. Nevertheless, "health care remains unaffordable for many middle-class people, who don't qualify for Medicaid or federal subsidies to help buy an individual policy. The average premium for a mid-level plan for a 40-year-old who doesn't qualify for a subsidy has climbed to $462 a month in 2020 from $273 in 2014, according to the Kaiser Family Foundation. And the law has done little to address soaring prescription drug costs and staggering deductibles."

Not only did a substantial number of individuals and families benefit from Obama care but also the health-care industry and insurance companies now had more customers and more steady revenue. According to the *New York Times,*

> After decades of carefully selecting whom
> they insured, insurers were forced to operate under
> the new requirement to offer anyone a policy, even

if that person had a potentially expensive medical condition, without charging a much higher price.

Many insurers suffered heavy losses at first. Some of the biggest players in health insurance abandoned the market. UnitedHealth Group, one of the nation's largest insurers, bowed out in 2016, citing losses of $1 billion. Lawmakers worried about so-called bare counties, places where insurers would simply refuse to offer coverage because there weren't enough customers or prices were too high to stay in business.

But while the learning curve was steep, insurers discovered how to prosper. They raised premiums enough to make money and narrowed their networks of hospitals and doctors to reduce their costs. Insurers also latched on to the government's Medicaid program, which is run by private insurers in most states.

The most glaring defect of Obamacare is the high deductibles of most plans before insurance coverage kicks in. Deductibles for individuals could reach $8,150 while for families may have to pay the first $16,300 before insurance coverage starts paying their medical bills.

The *Times* cites the case of Elizabeth Meyer of Chicago.

Meyer currently buys a health plan with a $6,650 deductible. She says she now goes to the doctor less than when she was uninsured, because she can no longer ask for a discount her providers typically gave to patients lacking coverage.

Another example of what could be the counterproductive ramifications of the ACA.

Jeremy Kridel, 43, lives in the Baltimore suburbs and buys coverage for his family through the health law marketplace. A federal subsidy brings the premium he pays down to $275 a month, but the plan's $13,000 family deductible means that the family frequently skips recommended care, including for his son who has autism.

So what are the better solutions to Obamacare's obvious flaws? According to *The Times*, "The health law's architects say there is an easy way to address the health law's large deductibles: pass new legislation that puts more money toward subsidies. Right now, the Affordable Care Act offers premium subsidies to Americans who earn up to 400 percent of the poverty line, about $48,500 for an individual and $100,000 for a family of four... Subsidies for deductibles go up only to 250 percent of the poverty line, meaning that families like Mr. Kridel's are excluded."

For Obamacare, the average monthly premium for a benchmark plan (the second lowest-cost silver plan) in 2020 is $388 for a twenty-seven-year-old enrollee and $1,520 for a family of four. If we use these numbers as a benchmark, what would it cost an individual and a family of four under an individual single-payer system?

The model that is applicable would be the same for individuals and families who receive employer-based insurance.

Individual Single-Payer Alternative for Obamacare Beneficiaries

Primary care	Approximately $125 monthly, tax-deductible cost for DPC or fee-for-service using a traditional doctor visit; estimated $300 for family of four.	Routine office visits and telemedicine and included blood tests
Health Savings Account	Tax-deductible initial deposit up to $20,000 or more; all deposits growing tax-free and withdrawn tax-free.	Specialists, prescription drugs, medical equipment major tests, such as mammography, colonoscopy, etc., and brief hospitalizations.
Catastrophic coverage / long-term care (facility or home based)	$1,000–$4,000 tax-deductible premium per annum based on age and medical conditions.	All major operations and hospitalizations. Long-term care in a facility would be paid from this account. There should be cost sharing to avoid overuse and fraud. Deductible could be as low as $1,000 and as high as $20,000 or more for individuals and families depending on their financial risk tolerance.

Figure 9

If the above chart looks familiar, it is essentially the same as the one in the previous chapter for employer-based insurance and in this chapter for Medicare beneficiaries. All the components are available in the marketplace, and therefore, we don't have to reinvent the wheel in order to have individuals and families be in total control of their medical care finances and with their physicians the appropriate decision-making for optimal health outcomes.

The evidence is so overwhelming that the current status quo of medical insurance is grossly overpriced and does not serve medical consumers as well as it should. For most individuals and families, access to a physician is the key to good health, and as we shall see in chapter 5, taking responsibility for one's health and focusing on wellness will keep medical costs down for households and in the aggregate, for the nation.

Chapter 4

Nonprofits and Voluntarism
Society's Successful Safety Net

Private philanthropy is the direct expression of the great
Christian principle of the brotherhood of man and the
Golden Rule. Private philanthropy indeed is the only valid
expression of these ethical principles; compulsory charity
through "social legislation" is the exact contrary: it is the
evil imposition of force by one group on another.

—Murray N. Rothbard

The old relationships of voluntary reciprocity and autonomy
have slowly given way to paternalistic dependency.

—David T. Beito

The success of the nonprofits undermines the
bureaucracy's power and denies its ideology.

—Peter F. Drucker

The American people have been bombarded with political
slogans ever since the trauma of the Great Depression began
ninety years ago. From FDR's New Deal, Truman's Fair
Deal, JFK's New Frontier, and LBJ's Great Society to Obama's Hope
and Change 2008 presidential campaign, which convinced enough

voters to elect him the nation's first African American president, the American people have been repeatedly told to put their trust in the federal government because "we are from the federal government and we are here to help you." Although Donald Trump's 2016 "Make America Great Again" campaign slogan helped him win the presidency by challenging the political establishment and confounding virtually all the pundits, he did not explicitly call for new federal government welfare programs and spending to deal with contemporary issues. On the contrary, his campaign touted repeal of the Affordable Care Act, which according to recent polls enjoys the support of the majority of the American people. But Trump did promise a "great" medical program to replace Obamacare.

Although Trump issued an executive order eliminating the tax penalty for not having medical insurance, the rest of the ACA remains intact. However, during the first three years of the Trump administration, he has maintained the status quo, as the "swamp" that he promised to drain is still consuming $4.4 trillion of the American people's income, the size of the 2019 federal budget which ended September 30, 2020. The 2020 federal budget ballooned to more than $7 trillion as the federal government has spent several trillion dollars to bailout virtually every sector of the economy and households as governors and mayor "locked down" their economies in response to the 2020 pandemic. Meanwhile, in the 2018 midterm election, several democratic socialists were elected and now are been promoting the "Green New Deal," which if fully implemented would give the federal government enormous control of the American people and the private sector, and turn the country into a full-blown fascistic/socialistic society.

But there is hope. Although the American people generally support America's welfare state—epitomized by Medicare, Medicaid, and a host of other "entitlement" program—which was born during FDR's New Deal and expanded under both Democratic and Republican administrations during the past nine decades, the intellectual opposition—economic and philosophical—to the welfare state has been extensive and indefatigable.

The welfare state violates a basic moral principle.

The so-called government safety net, in effect welfare spending, is "legal plunder," the term Frederick Bastiat coined in *The Law*, his classic defense of what the law should be in a free society. Bastiat described how to identify legal plunder:

> See if the law takes from some persons what belongs to them, and gives it to other persons to whom it does not belong. See if the law benefits one citizen at the expense of another by doing what the citizen himself cannot do without committing a crime.

Bastiat's solution: abolish the law as soon as possible because it is morally unacceptable in a free society to take money from Peter and give to Paul. He also chastised the proponents of legal plunder—which he argued is socialism—when he observed: "Socialism, like the ancient ideas from which it springs, confuses the distinction between government and society. As a result of this, every time we object to a thing being done by government, the socialists conclude that we object to its being done at all." In other words, applying Bastiat's insights about law, morality, and government spending to America's welfare state, focusing on Medicare and Medicaid (and CHIP), there are nongovernmental programs, institutions, organizations, etc. that would eliminate legal plunder and provide for more effective and less costly medical expenditures that would provide quality care for low-income households.

This is the theme of this chapter: creating a universal medical system that would address the needs of households with limited financial resources without the need for government to take from Peter and give to Paul. In other words, we can abolish legal plunder and reduce the inherent conflict that is created by the redistribution of income.

Critics of Social Welfarism

There have been scores of social scientists that have criticized the welfare state for more than one hundred years. An overview of that literature would fill at least one hefty volume. Some of the enduring critiques of the welfare state can be found, for example, several decades after Bastiat's *The Law* appeared in his native France; in America, Yale University sociologist William Graham Sumner wrote *What the Social Classes Owe to Each Other* (1883). He echoed many of Bastiat's observations when he wrote, "In a free society every man is held and expected to take care of himself and his family, to make no trouble for his neighbor, and to contribute his full share to public interest and common necessities." In short, he was arguing for laissez-faire, that is, in a free society "every man and woman in the society as one big duty. That is, to take care of his or her own self. This is a social duty." Sumner objected to what he called "social quackery," the notion that there must be a "plan" implemented by the political elites to deal with life's risks.

Did William Graham Sumner read *The Law*? If he did, then the following statement echoes Bastiat's opposition to legal plunder. "The state cannot get a cent for any man without taking it from some other man, and this latter must be a man who has produced and saved it." Sumner calls him the "Forgotten Man"—the man who works and saves and provides capital for the production of goods that the public wants. Sumner was calling for a very limited government that would be necessary for capital to be accumulated, which would then be used for the benefit of "society."

In 1969, Henry Hazlitt, one of the most prolific economic journalists and authors of the twentieth century, who was familiar with Bastiat's writings, because he was affiliated with the Foundation for Economic Education, which published an English version of *The Law* in 1950, contributed to a critique of the welfare state in *Man versus the Welfare State*. Hazlitt deviated from his usual laissez-faire perspective when he gave an example of how emergency medical care cannot be left to private charity. He asserts government should provide such care. However, he recognized, "the great problem is, of course, how to provide such emergency relief without allowing you to degenerate into permanent relief…"

As a classical liberal/libertarian, Hazlitt recognized that to establish or maintain a free society, the government must be limited. He wrote, "Only if the modern state can be held within a strictly limited agenda of duties and powers it can be prevented from recommending, conquering, and ultimately devouring the society which gave it birth. The solution to our problems is not more paternalism, laws, decrees, and controls, but the restoration of liberty and free enterprise, the restoration of incentives, to let loose the tremendous constructive energies of 200 million Americans." Now—fifty years later—of course, with more than 330 million Americans in the United States, the challenge is to offer practicable alternatives to the modern welfare state.

Currently, tens of millions of Americans are dependent upon the federal government for medical care after they turn sixty-five years old (Medicare), and more than 70 million poor and low-income individuals also rely on federal and state governments to subsidize their medical care (Medicaid). In other words, tens of millions of Americans are shirking their "social duty" as Sumner asserted, which is a prerequisite for a free society and harmonious relations among all classes in America. This is not to vilify the tens of millions of Americans who have come to rely on these programs to pay for their medical care. On the contrary, the beneficiaries of both Medicare and Medicaid are "rational" economic actors who, by law, are either required to participate in these programs (for example, Medicare Part A) or who have been "pulled into" the welfare state's safety net because the federal government has been co-opting the nonprofit sector with dozens of "entitlement" programs.

For all the reasons outlined above, there is a better way to provide medical care, especially to poor and low-income individuals and families, that doesn't violate the principles that Bastiat, Sumner, Hazlitt, Drucker, Mises, and Rothbard plus scores of other critics of the welfare state have articulated, namely, there is a moral imperative to create a free society. A free society would end legal plunder, encourage personal responsibility, be financially sustainable, and create an enhanced sense of community throughout the country.

Volunteers in Medicine

When Jack McConnell, MD, retired in 1989 after a distinguished career as a pharmaceutical executive with Johnson & Johnson and American Cyanamid's Lederle Laboratories, he thought he would spend his golden years playing golf in Hilton Head, South Carolina. To his dismay, he learned that many of the workers, from landscapers to waiters in the community, could not afford to pay for basic medical expenses. At the end of 1991, he and others were discussing the situation on Hilton Head when Dr. McConnell came up with the idea of a nonprofit medical center that would be staffed with volunteer retired physicians and other medical providers to deal with the needs of low-income workers in the community.

An obvious sticking point was malpractice insurance and licensing, inasmuch as many of the doctors were not from South Carolina, and therefore did not have the proper credentials to practice in the state. The state legislature grandfathered the volunteer doctors and insurance companies worked with the retired physicians to provide them adequate malpractice insurance. In 1997, the Federal Tort Claims Act began covering medical personnel in nonprofit health centers throughout the nation eliminating the need for separate malpractice insurance for doctors, nurses, and other health-care professionals.

The Hilton Head Volunteers in Medicine opened its doors in 1993 and a year later moved into a new building paid for by charitable contributions. As television reports of the nonprofit health center spread through the region and the nation, Dr. McConnell created Volunteers in Medicine to help local communities establish their own clinics. From its modest beginnings more than two decades ago, the Hilton Head Volunteers in Medicine (HHVIM) opened five days a week and has volunteer physicians specializing from cardiology to urology. In addition, the clinic provides ophthalmology services, weight management education, and other services to improve the health of the targeted population the clinic serves.

As the first of the current eighty-eight VIMs in the country, the clinic provided an estimated $13 million in medical benefits and 2018 and fifty-two thousand hours of patient services. Currently, the HHVIM has ten thousand active patients and more than twenty-seven thousand patient visits each year. The clinic estimates it saved local hospitals $6.8 million because the uninsured now have access to high-quality medical care with the cost per visit averaging $84. For its high-quality care and low-cost HHVIM for the fifth year in a row received the highest four-star rating from Charity Navigator.

The success of the Hilton Head Volunteers in Medicine clinic is a testament to Dr. McConnell's leadership and the commitment of the retired physicians and other health-care professionals in the mainly retirement community. This commitment is founded in the "Culture of Caring" vision. This culture treats each patient free of charge and without billing third-party payers. These principles articulated in the Volunteers in Medicine mission: "To promote, guide and help sustain a national network of free clinics emphasizing the use of retired medical and community volunteers within a culture of caring to improve access to health care for America's underserved and uninsured."

The VIM model establishes strong relationships with community stakeholders such as the medically underserved, local hospitals, and medical and nonmedical volunteers. In addition, to become a Volunteer in Medicine clinic, several minimum standards must be met. They include medical care to uninsured adults, no patient fees but donations are encouraged, no discrimination of any kind, no third-party billing, care is not dependent upon receiving a religious message, and the clinic must have a director who is a licensed independent practitioner in the state where the VIM is located.

According to the Volunteers in Medicine website, VIMs have proven the test of time as a model for local communities to create a medical facility for the uninsured throughout the country. The VIM Model is committed to providing quality patient care and ensuring that the medical professionals affiliated with a local medical center receive continuing education.

And with the "Culture of Caring" "the heart and soul of every VIM clinic," the fact that there are not thousands of VIMs across America as a reflection of how entrenched the welfare state is in the American psyche. The undeniable success of voluntary, non-profit medical centers based on the VIM model is another example of grassroots actions to deal with a major social issue—in this case medical care for the uninsured—that has been addressed throughout American history, namely, the generosity and kindness of professionals and volunteers.

The Volunteers in Medicine Fact Sheet contains additional information about the VIM Alliance that is expected to grow with twenty new sites in development. In 2018, nearly 87,000 patients were treated at VIM clinics, which provided more than 349,000 patient visits. VIM clinics reveal that the spirit of voluntarism is alive and well as more than ten thousand medical and nonmedical volunteers staffed the clinics around the country.

According to "diffusion theory," the idea of a nonprofit medical center would spread from its origin to nearby cities and neighboring states is evident in the location of VIMs. According to the fact sheet in addition to the increase of VIMs in South Carolina, which one would expect given how the idea took root in Hilton Head, VIMs have been created in Florida, Georgia, North Carolina, and several nearby states. In addition, eleven VIMs have been created in Pennsylvania, including two in Pittsburgh. In the country's most populous state, only four VIMs have been created in California and only one in New York, and that one is in upstate Oneonta. Texas has three clinics. All told there are VIMs in twenty-six states. In short, there is an enormous room for expansion for VIMs to all fifty states and most cities and towns, where the uninsured population could benefit from a nonprofit health center in their communities.

In 2018, the impact of Volunteers in Medicine cannot be overstated. Physicians treated hypertension, diabetes, mental health issues, and obesity as the most common diseases at the nonprofit medical clinics. In addition, on-site specialized services include pediatric care, dental services, and behavioral/mental health services. Moreover, nearly two-thirds of the clinics had off-site referrals, which numbered 37,606. Nearly three quarters of VIM Alliance clinics provide on-site pharmaceuticals or other methods to distribute medicines to patients.

Besides treating the uninsured or underinsured, 78 percent of VIM clinics use the facilities to help train medical and dental residents and physician assistants. In short, Volunteers in Medicine is a proven provider of medical care for the most vulnerable individuals and families in our communities and an invaluable resource for medical residents who are mentored by physicians who have devoted their lives to the medical profession.

Dr. Helmer of New Jersey who volunteers at two Garden State clinics, the Cape May county VIM and the Parker Family Health Center in Red Bank, sums up the efficacy of the Volunteers in Medicine model. "There is a spirit at Volunteers in Medicine that I have only felt at other VIM clinics. We are all connected by a cause and a belief that no one should have to do without basic health care and that little effort by each of us can make the world a better place for some money."

The Parker Family Health Center

The Parker Family Health Center is named after Dr. James Parker Sr. and his son Dr. James Parker Jr., who together served the Red Bank community for a total of eighty years beginning in 1919. The Parker Legacy is captured on the Health Center's website.

> Dr. Parker Sr. was born in Aiken, South Carolina, in 1888. His grandparents had both been born in slavery. A graduate of Howard University, James Sr., came to Red Bank in 1919, at the time of the influenza epidemic, and established his medical reputation treating flu victims. He cared for his patients in their homes,

because none of the local hospitals would accept an African-American doctor on their staff.

Dr. Parker Jr., born in Red Bank in 1919, followed his father first to Howard University and then into medicine. He opened his medical practice in his hometown in 1947, where he practiced until his retirement at the age of 82, with the only break his service in a front-line MASH unit in the US Army Medical Corps during the Korean War.

But Dr. Parker Jr., like his father before him, was best known for a medical practice that was open to all. He took care of generations of Red Bank residents, regardless of their background or ability to pay. He was renowned for opening his office doors at 5:00 AM so that his patients could see the doctor without missing work.

When Dr. Parker Jr.—then 80 years old— began thinking about retiring from practice, community members began wondering who would take care of the patients who had depended on him for so long.

West Side community leaders decided to take action. Among them was another leading African-American, Dr. Donald Warner, the recently retired superintendent of the Red Bank Regional School District and a 20-year friend of Dr. Parker. Dr. Warner, who is an ordained minister and a published poet, went door-to-door, asking West Side residents whether they had health insurance.

His findings were attention grabbing. Overall, 40 percent of West Side residents lacked health insurance. The worst off were members of a growing Latino community—95 percent uninsured. Most of the uninsured were in working families but employed in jobs that would not support increasingly costly health benefits.

Among those who paid attention to Donald Warner's survey was Dr. Eugene Cheslock, a local renowned oncologist also thinking about retirement from his active medical practice. His idea of retirement, however, was to start a free community clinic that would care for the uninsured with the help of medical volunteers.

Another local resident who paid attention was rock-and-roller Jon Bon Jovi. Early on, he and his wife, Dorothea, hosted a gala at their home that raised the funds for the construction of a permanent clinic building. Later, a local high school asked him to perform in a charity concert to benefit the clinic. He said yes, and the students raised $60,000 for Parker's prescription medication fund. The concert, an acoustic performance, drew the attention of music lovers all over the world and led to a feature about the Parker Center on ABC-TV's *20/20* news program.

The clinic envisioned by Dr. Gene Cheslock and Dr. Donald Warner, which would be named the Parker Family Health Center in honor of the two doctors, opened in a converted trailer parked in an empty lot on Shrewsbury Avenue, just down the street from Dr. Parker's office. Clinic staff saw three patients on that first night.

The Parker Family Health Center continues to serve as an initial health-care access point, making it possible for uninsured patients to establish the routine relationship with a medical caregiver that insured patients enjoy with a primary physician. Like the primary physician, the Parker Family Health Center provides referrals for specialty care, one of the most significant hurdles for the uninsured, through a network of specialists who volunteer regularly at the clinic, representing some twenty medical disciplines. Diagnostic testing is also available through Riverview Medical Center and other resources. Affordable prescription drugs—another costly hurdle for the uninsured—are filled either through pharmacy assistance programs for eligible patients or at three local drugstores that have agreed to fill prescriptions from the clinic formulary at negotiated prices.

Like the Drs. Parker, father and son, the clinic that bears their name and sees anyone who does not have health insurance and has limited means to pay for care. Among the eight thousand clinic patients are many African Americans who are longtime residents of Red Bank's West Side. Others include newer West-Siders from Latino neighborhoods, Portuguese-speaking members of a Brazilian community in nearby Long Branch, and anyone else without insurance from anywhere in Monmouth County.

Currently, the Parker family Health Center has approximately 2,000 patients, and in 2018, the center had 6,444 patient visits slightly more than 2017 but more than 1,300 less than 2015. The drop in patients is due to the enactment of the Affordable Care Act and patients who bought insurance through the government created marketplace. However, the high cost of insurance because many patients to come back to the Parker Family Health Center. In addition, patients could not keep the doctors as promised, and many specialists were unavailable on those plans. Although the ACA was touted as an affordable way to decrease the number of uninsured in the country, according to the Parker Family Health Center director, Mary Nicosia, the center has been a lifeline for their patients.

The Parker Center has seven full-time staff and approximately thirty volunteers per week who put in the 120 hours weekly to help run the center. The nearest hospital provides blood work pro bono for the center's patients, and most of the uninsured patients that are discharged from the emergency room are encouraged to become patients.

The Parker Family Center does not have a development/public relations department and in 2020 hired an executive director; it does not have personnel for outreach or the funds to advertise. Nevertheless, the approximately $1 million budget of which 75 percent to 80 percent is for staff salaries and benefits, provides excellent care for its two thousand active patients. The Center could handle more patients but does not actively seek them.

Suzanne Dyer, Parker's new ED, provide the following update regarding several initiatives that are underway to provide additional services to its patients.

> [We introduced new initiatives such as] Athenahealth (an electronic medical records platform), Telehealth, and Uberhealth (to assist

patients with transportation at no cost to them). Under normal circumstances, each of these initiatives would require a year to research, negotiate and implement. As it is, Parker is rolling out all three in a matter of months. Even more importantly, Parker has managed to secure funding for all three ventures.

These programs will allow Parker to expand its provision of healthcare and increase access throughout the county by eliminating two significant obstacles for the patient: lack of transportation (Uberhealth) and fear of exposure to COVID-19 (Telehealth).

Athenahealth, our third initiative, is an electronic medical records (EMR) system which will allow Parker to replace its existing paper chart system. Although this electronic system will bring a much welcome upgrade to the clinic, Parker still needs to be mindful of the many older, retired volunteer providers critical to Parker's success. Many of these providers find the concept of EMRs daunting and are not interested in mastering a new computer program at this stage of their careers. With this challenge in mind, Parker will employ a medical scribe. Primarily, the scribe will be assigned to this particular group of providers and will work in the examining room with the provider when the provider is on site. The scribe can also conference in with the provider when the provider engages a patient through telehealth.

Parker strives to focus on preventative and primary care. Services include an established pediatric program which treats 5 to 18-year-olds. This program provides vaccinations, school and employment physicals, and dental care for children under the age of 14. The current Women's

Health program provides treatment on site for women experiencing gynecological issues while well women visits and diagnostics are referred off site to partner organizations. This program is being revised to bring well women visits back to Parker.

The majority of Parker patients, however, suffer from chronic disease, i.e. hypertension, diabetes, and/or both. Consistent with national statistics for underserved populations, Parker's patients are, at minimum, 24% more likely to suffer from diabetes than others because of the environment they live in and the social determinants they face on a daily basis. Also, over 50% of Parker patients are diagnosed with hypertension. In addition to upgrading its operational systems, Parker is also revising its medical care services, striving to address underlying causes of these chronic diseases which include food scarcity, lack of housing, financial insecurity, and emotional stress. Parker's on-site social worker works with patients to determine which social determinants these patients face and what solutions might be available.

With this holistic approach to care, addressing both medical and non-medical problems in the course of treatment, Parker seeks to not only treat the disease but also the underlying causes that can prevent optimal health.

Patients with chronic diseases stay with the clinic until they move away or get jobs with medical insurance, which is rare. Patients with acute problems usually only return as needed. It is difficult to convince them to return for wellness visits because many patients in the Red Bank area are struggling to make ends meet and have a difficult time with follow-up visits to treat the most common elements hypertension and diabetes.

The addition of a full-time executive director has been a huge boon to the growth of the Parker Family Health Center who has been instrumental in fundraising and having a greater impact in Monmouth County, whether centers located in addition the center wants to increase its primary care and specialty physicians, nurses, and nurse practitioners and interpreters. Approximately 60 percent of the center's patients are Hispanic.

According to Mary Nicosia, the Center's clinical director,

> The VIM model works well because the many retired doctors can continue to practice in a welcoming and much needed environment. Many retired doctors have not developed 'retirement activities' and want to still practice what they do best-medicine. The hospitals are appreciative that we are keeping primary care and non-emergency patients out of their emergency rooms. And keeping chronically ill patients from the devastating outcomes of the complications of unmanaged disease. Not just physicians, but many of our volunteers are retired individuals that are sharing their expertise in many ways. The philosophy of the medical community, including nurses and nurse practitioners is in alignment with the mission of VIM and the talent that these individuals bring to our clinics is priceless. The FTCA (Federal Tort Claims Act) which covers the malpractice of many of the VIM clinics is a government sponsored program from HRSA that is well designed to assure that the clinics practice safely. It requires policies and procedures and multiple levels of practitioner checks to guarantee public safety. This is a great savings on medical malpractice insurance.

In addition to these two New Jersey clinics, there is one in Forked River and Hackensack. The inspiration for creating the Hackensack facility, the Bergen Volunteer Medical Initiative (BVMI. org), is similar to the creation of the first VMI in Hilton Head.

Bergen Volunteer Medical Initiative

Dr. Sam Cassell, a Fair Lawn internist, retired in 2001 expecting to enjoy his golden years playing bridge and traveling. When he was on vacation the Far East, he assisted bringing a young Vietnamese girl to get free medical treatment in the United States. He also participated a medical mission to Haiti. Dr. Sam, as he was affectionately known, became committed to voluntarism. In subsequent conversations with other medical professionals, he discovered Volunteers in Medicine. Dr. Sam and other physicians from Bergen County met with the founder of the Parker Family Health Center, Dr. Eugene Cheslock in Red Bank. From that meeting, Dr. Sam and others committed themselves to creating a nonprofit medical center in Bergen County.

After several years of planning, BVMI opened its doors as a licensed ambulatory center in 2009 and moved to its new facility, the Lynn Diamond Healthcare Center, a five-thousand-square-foot clinic in Hackensack in March 2017.

The following Fact Sheet highlights BVMI's Commitment to serving a population in one of the most prosperous counties in the nation—a community one would not think there would be a need for nonprofit, free health-care center. But the facts reveal why there is a need for a nonprofit health center in southern Bergen County and how BVMI has marshaled community resources that would make Bastiat, Sumner, Hazlitt, and others proud who advocated voluntarism as the ethical and most effective method to deal with medical needs of low-income individuals and families.

Fact Sheet

BVMI provides free primary, urgent, preventive and chronic care to low-income working Bergen County residents who do not have medical insurance. Individuals/families may earn up to 250 percent of the federal poverty level. More than 80,000 adults under the age of 65 in Bergen County are uninsured (census.gov).

Bergen County is one of the ten most prosperous counties in the nation with a per capita income of $46,601, and a median household income of $91,572. Despite this wealth, 6.6% of the County's residents live below the federal poverty level. Fifteen percent of Bergen County adults earning less than 250% of the Federal Poverty Level do not have health insurance (Henry J. Kaiser Family Foundation).

BVMI is a licensed, ambulatory healthcare center. In March 2017, BVMI relocated to the new Lynn Diamond Healthcare Center, a 5,000 square foot facility in Hackensack, NJ. Patients are seen by appointment five days a week. In 2019, BVMI provided more than 9,200 medical visits for 1,525 patients. The patient census increased by 65% in three years.

A team of 75 volunteer physicians, nurse practitioners, registered nurses and other healthcare professionals provide medical care for BVMI's patients. More than 200 specialists in private practice in the county have agreed to see BVMI patients at no charge.

All five Bergen County hospitals provide x-rays and advanced diagnostic procedures for BVMI patients. BD provides donated medical products, and Quest Diagnostics provides comprehensive laboratory services. J&J Pharmacy in Teaneck, NJ provides discounted medicines to patients and donates supplies to the Healthcare Center.

Through early intervention and consistent treatment of patients, BVMI has been able to stabilize chronic conditions, help reduce infectious disease and decrease Emergency Room visits.

BVMI focuses on improving health literacy and expanding access to healthcare for underserved communities by providing primary care, sick and chronic care through the Diabetes Patient Care and Education Program and the Women's Health Initiative. A new Prevent Diabetes Program launched in January, 2019, and a new Korean Healthcare Program began in September, 2018. Many corporate and foundation donors have made this possible, including the Aetna Foundation, Russell Berrie Foundation, Horizon Foundation for New Jersey, The Kaplen Foundation, Korean American Community Foundation, OritaniBank Foundation, TD Bank, the Luckow Family Foundation and the Taub Foundation.

BVMI does not receive any government funding, is not reimbursed by insurance companies and does not charge patients for services provided. BVMI relies entirely on contributions from individuals, corporations and foundations. (Emphasis added)

The fact sheet does not fully capture the enormous success of BVMI, which is located in Hackensack, the county seat, and sees patients from nearly every one of the seventy municipalities in Bergen County. BVMI has a $2,000,000 annual budget, twenty-eight paid employees, and seven full-time and twenty part-time staffers who are committed to patients' receiving excellent medical care during the five days that the center is open. Nurse practitioners plus the volunteer doctors treat thirty-five to forty patients a day at BVMI.

According to Amanda Missy, president and CEO of BVMI, the long-term plan for the center is to have its own building and satellite offices in other towns where there are thousands of individuals and families need medical care. In addition, BVMI would like to provide dental services to its patients, some of whom have not seen a dentist for as long as twenty years.

Missy pointed out in a June 2019 interview at BVMI that patients routinely spend at least an hour with the physician or nurse practitioner in the initial visit and at least thirty minutes in follow-up visits compared with shorter visits at the federally subsidized Federal Qualified Health Centers (FQHC), where patients typically also see a nurse practitioner or a physician.[18]

Zarephath Health Center

With an annual budget of approximately $60,000 a year, the Zarephath Health Center founded (2003) by doctors John and Alieta Eck is located in Somerset, New Jersey (Somerset County). The ZHC was created after the Ecks after they visited the Parker Family Health Center in the early 2000s and met with founder Dr.

---

[18] The FQHCs…are safety net providers that primarily provide services typically furnished in an outpatient clinic. FQHCs include community health centers, migrant health centers, health care for the homeless health centers, public housing primary care centers, and health center program "look-alikes." They also include outpatient health programs or facilities operated by a tribe or tribal organization or by an urban Indian organization. FQHCs are paid based on the FQHC Prospective Payment System (PPS) for medically necessary primary health services and qualified preventive health services furnished by an FQHC practitioner.

For a comprehensive overview of how FQHCs differ from VIMS see the structure and operations of these medical centers (https://www.cms.gov/Outreach-and-Education/Medicare-Learning-Network-MLN/MLNProducts/Downloads/FQHC-Text-Only-Factsheet.pdf).

Gene Cheslock. The Ecks were impressed with Dr. Cheslock's commitment to quality health care without government interference for the poor and uninsured in their community, they may immediately planned to open a nonprofit medical center in the community.

Initially housed in a nine-hundred-square-foot building, ZHC moved to a five-thousand-square-foot building across the street from its original location several years ago. The new facility has three intake rooms, five exam rooms, and a classroom.

ZHC is a faith-based nonprofit medical center. Thus, it is not affiliated with Volunteers in Medicine. Nevertheless, according to its website, "The Zarephath Health Center represents an example of faith in action. It provides a venue for professionals and other volunteers to use their gifts in practical ways by giving people who have fallen into hard times a way out. We believe that being uninsured does not have to be a cause for despair but can be an opportunity for others to reach out and help." In other words, it is a volunteer medical center based upon the model of the Good Samaritan, which effectively is the ethical foundation of Volunteers in Medicine, helping those in need in our community based upon the "culture of caring."

The ZHC is open only twelve hours per week and has approximately three hundred patients who make approximately 2,400 visits annually. There are no full-time employees, three paid part-time staff members, and all the doctors and nurses volunteer their time to see patients at the center. Neighboring hospitals refer patients to ZHC but do not provide much financial support. Fundraising efforts are minimal. A fundraising letter is sent once a year to its donor base, and many supporters donate monthly.

The passage of the ACA caused a small drop in patient visits. However, at this time, half the patients the center sees are on Medicaid but cannot find a physician who will take them on as patients. The center does not advertise for patients, some of whom were referred by hospitals or psychiatric facilities and have learned about the center by word-of-mouth.

The center's budget does not pose a challenge to serve the uninsured, but more physicians are needed to volunteer in order for the center to be open more than twelve hours per week. In addition, direct relief donates thousands of dollars in medicine per month, and people donate crutches, commodes, and other durable medical equipment that we donate to patients.

One of the greatest challenges for the center is losing patients who visit once or twice and then do not follow up on their visits. Fortunately, some patients obtain insurance when they find a new job.

Like most nonprofit medical centers for the uninsured, they treat patients for hypertension, diabetes, heart disease, bronchitis, pneumonia, psychiatric illnesses, chronic pain, and various addictions. In addition, the center helps patients get surgery but are unable to be treated through the Medicaid system.

The center's long-term goal is to "multiply the concept." Dr. Eck hope to see the passage NJS-239, "Doctors who donate four hours per week [to nonprofit health centers] would get medical malpractice coverage in their private practices provided by the state."

The Zarephath Health Center is undoubtedly one of the most cost-effective nonprofits in the country. And according to cofounder Dr. Alieta Eck, "Nothing is more efficient than real charity—where people volunteer and the transaction is complete when the patient leaves the clinic. No billing, no coding and claims production, and no money going from the government to providers who provide charity care. With our charity concept, there is no possibility for fraud or the waste of taxpayer dollars. It would save billions of federal and state dollars currently squandered in the Medicaid system."

The Path to a National Nonprofit Medical Care Strategy

Dr. Jack McConnell, Drs. John and Alieta Eck, Dr. Gene Cheslock, and countless others throughout the United States have created medical centers to provide care for low-income individuals and families in their respective communities. Their selfless acts are a testimony to the enormous goodwill and compassion of physicians and other volunteers to deal with ongoing medical needs without depending on taxpayers' dollars. The success of their nonprofit, donor-financed centers belies the notion that Medicaid is necessary to provide medical care for underserved segments of the population.

The challenge for our comprehensive single-payer system is to provide a blueprint for phasing out Medicaid and substituting a national network of nonprofit medical centers funded solely by charitable contributions. The transition has, in fact, already begun without any systematic planning or without anyone realizing that nonprofit charitable centers would be replacing Medicaid in the years ahead.

Currently, there are at least 1,400 Free Health Clinics according to the National Association of Free and Charitable Clinics (Nfac. org), an organization founded in 2001 to promote the nonprofit medical center model as a viable safety net health-care organization. The NAFC has also under its umbrella nonprofits that "charge a nominal/sliding fee to patients."

The association received the huge boost when it and Dr. Oz held the free health clinic in Houston, Texas (2009). In just one day, 1,800 uninsured city and other residents received care, which was filmed and turned into a one-hour television show. National media picked up the story of the uninsured, and subsequently one day, free clinics were held in sixteen other cities across the country. Nearly nineteen thousand uninsured individuals received care, and more than seventeen thousand volunteers participated in the one-day free clinics.

Despite the passage of the affordable care act that was hailed as a necessary program to increase insurance coverage for tens of millions of Americans, nearly thirty million Americans are still uninsured. But as it is been argued in previous chapters, the American people are "overinsured" and that to restore the doctor-patient relationship and provide high-quality care at reasonable cost to the vast majority of Americans, we need a different medical care "model."

The NAFC has been leading the way to expand medical coverage for the underserved throughout the country by partnering with CVS Health and the CVS Health Foundation. In 2020, for example, $2 million in grants or provided by the aforementioned organizations to expand telehealth services in free and charitable clinics and pharmacies. And CVS Health launched a $500,000 multiyear grant program for Free and Charitable Clinics in Ohio.

In July 2019, the NAFC received a $2.9 million grant from CVS Health and its foundation to support nearly 130 Free and Charitable Clinics throughout the country as part of their commitment to increase access to quality care in communities across the country. The grants range from $10,000 to $20,000 each.

Currently, there are more than 9,900 CVS store throughout America. Walgreens has nearly 9,300 stores. Walmart has nearly 4,800 stores. Home Depot nearly 2,000 stores. Lowe's has approximately 2,000 stores, and Costco just under 600 stores. All told there are more than 28,000 locations throughout America in virtually every urban and rural community that could house a nonprofit center to provide basic medical care for current Medicaid patients. Even if only one-third of those locations would be viable for one reason or another, to locate a nonprofit medical center, that would still leave more than 9,000 locations available to provide medical care. If each location would partner with a new local Voluntary in Medicine organization or any other free clinic model, eight thousand patients per new nonprofit medical center would begin the transition away from Medicaid. All seventy-million-plus Medicaid and CHIP beneficiaries would receive their primary care at one of these locations. Patients of the nonprofits would get specialized medical services such as mammograms, colonoscopies, etc. from physician volunteers at these locations or paid for by donations. Local hospitals would provide the charity care as they do now throughout the country. Hospitals would undertake charity care drives to raise the funds necessary to meet the needs of the local population.

For every pharmacy and big-box store that carves out space and spends, let's say, $200,000 to outfit such a nonprofit medical center, that amount would be a tax credit on the businesses—federal tax return. Thus, the initial capital expenditure for each nonprofit center would be "costless" to CVS, Walgreens, etc. as their federal tax liability would be lowered by the amount they invest in every medical facility.

The medical personnel and administrative staff needed to run a center could be tapped from the nearly one million active physicians in the United States who would could be on the front lines so to speak volunteering, let's say, five to ten hours per week at each center. In addition, several hundred thousand retired physicians also could volunteer providing a huge pool for these centers around the country.

To pay for administrative staff personnel, each center would undertake a fundraising campaign, and a federal tax credit would be granted to any individual or business that makes a donation to a nonprofit medical center. This proposal is in keeping with Drucker's observation in his *Wall Street Journal* essay, "It Profits Us to Strengthen Nonprofits," that to increase the incentive for donations to nonprofits, individuals should get a $1.10 deduction for every dollar they donate. Our proposal provides a huge incentive to donate to nonprofits by writing off $1.00 in tax liability for every dollar donated.

Would not every taxpayer in America want to reduce his or her tax liability, and have those funds instead go to a local nonprofit medical center to serve low-income households? Private charity, in other words, would be in keeping with Murray Rothbard's statement in the opening of this chapter, namely, is an ethical act of individual compassion. Moreover, phasing out Medicaid and replacing it with a network of nonprofit centers would reduce bureaucratic management of medical care in this country for low-income households. Thus, the only "losers" in our proposal would be the bureaucracy staffed by well-meaning but unnecessary individuals who have unleashed a torrent of rules and regulations that stifle the practice of medicine.

At the West Virginia Health Right (WVHR) center, which has been serving patients since 1982 in Charleston, CEO nurse practitioner Angie Settle was quoted in an NAFC essay about the clinic, "I think free and charitable clinics are the most overlooked jewel of the US." Settle make some additional points about the patients: "A lot of people have this misconception about free clinics that it's just a handout for people who don't want to work. That can't be further from the truth. 83% of our patients are employed in some capacity." In addition, she points out, "Without us, a lot of people that we see would have no alternative but to turn to public assistance, to quit the job so they can get poor enough to be on Medicaid."

A nurse practitioner at WVHR points out that clinic patients can see a specialist relatively quick as opposed to waiting six months to a year participating in a federal program such as Medicaid.

One of the main benefits for patients at the clinic is attending wellness classes, where healthy cooking, diabetes management, and exercise are in great demand. This is important component of the clinic's mission because West Virginia is often cited as America's unhealthiest state.

A fifty-seven-year-old West Virginia says about the clinic, "I would literally be dead without this clinic."

The evidence around the country from nonprofit medical centers is overwhelmingly they are providing quality medical care. Creating enough centers is doable for all Medicaid patients by scaling up the locations to transition the seventy-one million Medicaid beneficiaries. The greater challenge is the funding necessary to pay for Medicaid recipients in nursing homes, which currently is approximately $30 billion annually.

For the time being, these funds could be paid out of general revenue for the next five to ten years as a transition to a nonprofit medical care model for low-income individuals in nursing homes. During the transition, private nursing homes that receive Medicaid funding for residents would have to create a separate nonprofit entity that would raise the funds for low-income individuals. The nonprofit nursing homes would raise the funds from donors who would receive a dollar tax credit for every dollar donated to the new 501(c)(3) nursing home.

A less costly solution would be for low-income individuals to receive as much care as possible at home instead of a relatively expensive nursing facility. The goal, therefore, for end-of-life care should be to provide compassionate, quality care at reasonable costs to the elderly and others who need to reside in a nursing home.

Long-term, the pool of funds for newborns would pay for this care sixty, seventy, eighty years or more in the future. As this pool of funds increases over many decades, the cohort of newborns that go through life together would have a substantial reservoir of resources to pay for nursing home care. Ideally, the need for nursing homes would decline markedly for babies born in the 2020s and beyond the twenty-first century. That goal could be achieved by focusing on wellness and personal responsibility, which will be discussed in the next chapter.

In the meantime, home care would have to become more wide-spread for those seniors who could have a relatively high quality of life outside a nursing home in the last years of life.

The challenge to the American people is, Do you want to see low-income individuals and households receive high-quality medical care at no cost to taxpayers? The question is rhetorical. Insofar, as there is no free lunch, the cost-effective nonprofit medical centers would need the support of tens of millions Americans in order to provide such care and reduce Medicaid spending by nearly $600 billion annually.

Will the American people step up to the plate and create the network of nonprofit medical centers that would solve a major social issue? Time will tell if the American people are in fact as compassionate as they claim to be and are willing to use voluntary means at the grassroots level to help their fellow neighbors.

Chapter 5

Wellness, Optimal Health and Personal Responsibility

Health is a state of complete physical, mental and social well-being and not merely the absence of disease or infirmity.
—Preamble to the World Health Organization Constitution

Wellness is not a part-time job. 80% of chronic conditions are controllable through lifestyle measures.
—Glenn Gero, ND

Is it your responsibility to take care of yourself or is it that of other people?
—Michael Rozeff

Healthy eating is one of the most powerful tools we have to reduce the onset of disease.
—Academy of Nutrition & Dietetics

Personal responsibility—and accountability—is one of the essential characteristics of a civilized society. Peaceful relations—respect for property and individual rights—among all peoples would create social harmony based on voluntary exchange. A limited government—as envisioned in our Bill of Rights—would protect individual rights, and local and state governments would prosecute transgressors in a court of law.

Criminals are responsible for their actions. Business owners are responsible for the quality of their products and services. Elected official are accountable to the voters throughout the year and on Election Day. Adults are accountable to their spouses, children, and parents. Physicians are responsible for doing no harm to their patients. We are all held accountable and responsible no matter what our income is, what profession we have chosen to practice, what neighborhood we live in. No other being, whether he is a government official, corporate executive, religious leader, etc., is responsible for the day-to-day decisions a human being has to make to live in a "state of well-being." We human beings have free will to act according to our values, preferences likes/dislike, etc. And we are—or should be—held accountable for all our actions. And that includes our state of well-being.

Who then is responsible for an individual's health care and well-being? The honest/correct answer is, every individual is responsible for his/her state of health. Health is a very personal matter. Nevertheless, there is a common theme, as we shall see in this chapter, that should create a more healthy population and reduce the chronic problems that cause pain and suffering among tens of millions of Americans. And let's not forget the $3.6 trillion that is spent on medical care—funds that could be used for better housing, education, and other goods and services.

The assertion that "health care is a right" confuses health care with medical care. We are responsible for our well-being while medical care is a service we seek to address an illness that is sudden, life-threating, and requires a trained medical doctor or other practitioner to diagnose our condition and prescribe a treatment.

The notion that health care / medical care is the same as the right to free, speech, assembly, religion, bearing arms, and other rights enumerated in the Bill of Rights is grossly erroneous.

The rights outlined in the Bill of Rights are "negative." That is, the government does not have a right *to interfere* with our freedom of speech, freedom of assembly, freedom of religion, etc. These rights do not obligate the government to provide us with the means to exercise our rights, such as a newspaper, radio show, house of worship, a firearm, etc.

Health care /medical care is like any other service we need and desire; the law of supply and demand would balance the needs of individuals with the supply of doctors, hospitals, etc., if we had a free market in medical care. But we don't. Instead, we have elements of free markets with the heavy hand of government interfering with the needs of patients and the supply of medical care.

Prices, in a free market, reflect the relative scarcity or abundance of a particular service or product. Collectivists, however, assert people cannot "shop" for medical services when they are in an automobile accident, having a heart attack or stroke. Good point, but irrelevant. People should arrange their affairs so when an emergency occurs, they do not have to worry about payment for medical services when a tragedy occurs.

In this chapter, we begin with the prospective of Dr. Glenn Gero, who was interviewed in his Clifton, New Jersey, office. He spoke about his decades long journey from an unhealthy preteen to a highly regard naturopathic doctor.

*****

Twelve-year-old Fair Lawn, New Jersey resident Glenn Gero was very overweight. One day, he overheard two adults talking, and one of them said, "Look how fat that boy is." Instead of running home and sulking about his obesity and complaining to his parents about the "bullying" he experienced, Glenn took responsibility for his condition at age twelve; he went on a lifelong mission to achieve optimal health and well-being.

Although Glenn did not seek his parents' guidance nor did he ask them to take him to the family physician to get treated for his obesity, he immersed himself in learning about diet, nutrition, and exercise and spent a good portion of his paper route money on weights and "muscle" magazines. His father complained to Glenn about the barbells in the garage, but Glenn insisted that the barbells be allowed to stay there so he can undertake his weight training routine. A year later, he had lost enough weight to enter a track meet, and for a very brief moment held, his middle school record for the sixty-yard dash until the next heat of boys ran the same race. *Sic transit gloria.*

Sixty years after tackling his obesity, Glenn Gero is one of the most sought-after naturopaths in the state of New Jersey and has been in private practice for more than two decades with thousands of patients seeking his advice for a variety of ailments. So how did Gero's preteen weight problem, which he was able to overcome with determination and self-help, turn eventually into a health-care career helping individuals achieve the goals stated in the WHO Constitution preamble?

Dr. Gero opened his naturopathic practice in 2001. He is a board-certified naturopathic physician who has earned three master's degrees and two doctorates and over twenty certifications in various disciplines of natural medicine, including those in medical exercise, biofeedback, botanical medicine, and holistic health coaching.

Dr. Gero has completed postdoctoral training at Harvard Medical School, Johns Hopkins School of Medicine, and Columbia College for Physicians and Surgeons. He had held executive medical publishing positions with the *American Journal of Surgery*, *The American Journal of Cardiology*, and with the *American College of Physicians* and had served as a regional vice president of the American Heart Association. He is a professional member of the Harvard Medical School Post-graduate Association and had served as an adjunct professor at the New York College of Podiatric Medicine.

Although Gero was on a mission to maintain a normal body weight, eat right, and exercise to have optimal health, he did not choose to go to medical school to become physician, who most individuals consider the professional that would cure their illnesses and provide guidance for optimal health. Three decades ago, Gero learned that conventional, orthodox medicine is not infallible and that a visit to a naturopath three decades ago would change his pursuit of optimal well-being forever and set him on a course to become a health-care professional.

Feeling run-down with low energy, Glenn Gero visited several physicians who told him "everything is okay" even though they did not do any comprehensive "health inventory" of his condition. Some even suggested, "It's all in your head." Obviously frustrated, Glenn saw an ad in a directory for a naturopathic doctor in Asbury Park. At the first visit, the ND recommended a detoxification program, supplements, and changes to his diet. A blood test revealed Glenn had wheat sensitivity. After several weeks of following the naturopath's recommendations, Glenn felt immeasurably better by maintaining an appropriate, individualized dietary program.

Glenn had a very successful publishing business but decided to pursue his lifelong passion. Hence, in the 1990s, he decided to become a naturopathic doctor and provide individuals with information he felt they were not getting from conventional physicians. He enrolled in a full-time course of study to earn his naturopathic degree. His education has been augmented by countless continuing education sessions at the prestigious institutions mentioned previously. At Harvard University, for example, Gero has completed two years of conventional medical training both on campus and online.

How do naturopathic approaches differ from conventional medical practices? According to Gero, conventional medicine focuses on suppressing symptoms while the naturopath primarily focuses on what is causing a patient's symptoms. Naturopathic doctors are trained in anatomy, physiology, pathology, and many other science disciplines that are taught in medical school. Additionally, naturopathic doctors receive extensive training in lifestyle medicine, nutrition, botanical medicine, and other safe natural therapies, which seek to discover the imbalances in a patient's body, not least of which are the food sensitivities that may be adversely affecting an individual's optimal well-being.

Medical school students receive virtually no nutrition instruction. A recent National Institute for Health (NIH) report has revealed that, on average, students only received 23.9 contact hours of nutrition instruction during medical school (range: two to seventy hours). Only forty schools required the minimum twenty-five hours recommended by the National Academy of Sciences. During one of Dr. Gero's lectures at Rutgers Medical School, he asked the students how much nutrition training they received. They responded, "About two hours in one afternoon."

A major criticism of conventional medical practices, according to Gero, is that medical schools derive 40 percent of their funding from pharmaceutical company contributions. Glenn asserts this is a major conflict of interest and cites as proof the dearth of nutritional training medical students receive. In 2005, this acknowledgment created a full-blown movement. He points out, however, that Harvard Medical School is not dependent on pharmaceutical funding because of their huge endowment. Gero believes this should serve as a model for all medical schools. They should not rely on "special interest" funding to train their students. In addition, he believes medical students would be better served as well as their future patients if they learned "integrative medicine." That is, using the strengths of both conventional medicine and naturopathic approaches to treating the patient.

As a newly minted naturopathic doctor, Glenn Gero opened his office in April 2001. He began with a sign outside his Clifton, New Jersey, office and placed ads in the local magazines he was still publishing to attract patients. After three years, Glenn had a viable practice, which maintains liability and malpractice insurance. He soon sold the publishing business to concentrate full-time on his new career.

Since Gero received his degree, he has pursued a rigorous continuing education program, especially by attending seminars about cancer in addition to a four-day week practice where he sees about a half a dozen patients a day. Currently, he sees patients with digestive issues, which is a huge part of his practice, suffer from chronic fatigue and autoimmune problems such as rheumatoid arthritis, MS, and lupus. Some of his patients have not been able to obtain relief from conventional medical treatments and are looking for "alternatives" to orthodox approaches to treat their ailments. Glenn estimates that about 70 percent of his patients are not satisfied with conventional medicine while the other 30 percent believe he can help them heal using protocols such as diet, supplements, and exercise.

As Gero's practice has grown, so has his reputation. Patients have seen relief from the debilitating conditions they have suffered before being treated by him. By word of mouth, information on his website, and internet searches, he now sees one to three new cancer patients per week. In fact, Gero works closely with medical doctors to make sure the protocols he is recommending is not in conflict with the physicians' treatments. Glenn states that his "relationship is better than ever with physicians." Doctors are realizing there is more to wellness than just prescribing medication.

Dr. Gero believes his relationship with physicians is strong because, as he puts it, "I speak their language." Recently, medical doctors have requested they have the opportunity to "shadow" him in his office to learn his best practices as a naturopathic doctor.

One of Gero's major concerns as reported in *the Journal of the American Medical Association* regarding conventional medicine is sobering: one hundred thousand deaths each year due to individuals taking pharmaceutical drugs as directed. He points out that a widely used over-the-counter pain relief medicine causes sixteen thousand deaths per year because of liver toxicity. For Glenn, this is personal. His mother died of liver toxicity after taking this widely used anti-inflammatory over-the-counter medicine at the direction of her physician. Glenn was unaware of his mother's continuous use of this highly popular medication.

So what does Gero do to assist his patients improve their well-being and achieve optimal health? More and more of his patients have endocrine issues, which throws the body's chemistry off-balance and leads to a host of ailments. To determine the nature of an individual's imbalances, he analyzes their blood chemistry—a key part of his practice. Glenn believes a comprehensive blood workup is crucial to determining what protocols he could recommend to his patients. He claims doctors are not adequately trained to read blood chemistry, a flaw he believes is a result of their medical education.

For example, one of Gero's patients was at least one hundred pounds overweight. The patient followed his recommendations after analyzing his blood chemistry and lost one hundred pounds in ten months—one of many success stories he is proud to share.

Dr. Gero consults regularly with oncologists, whose patients are also seeking his advice. He is appalled that dietitians recommend sugary snacks after chemotherapy session. Glenn says this is "insane." He points out that sugar causes cancer cells to proliferate. The nutritional ignorance of oncologists, other specialists, and dietitians harms patients, according to Glenn. Dietitians recommend cancer patients bulk up with sugary foods, which is precisely the wrong protocol for them. So why has not this information trickled in from naturopaths to the medical profession?

Several years ago, one of Gero's patients was diagnosed with fourth-stage pancreatic cancer and was told she had three months to live. After the patient visited her oncologist and told her tumor markers were down 70 percent, the patient thanked the oncologist who told her, "Don't thank me. Thank your naturopath." The patient lived for another three and a half years and had a relatively comfortable end-of-life journey thanks to Glenn Gero's naturopathic training.

When new patients meet Gero, they fill out a sixteen-page questionnaire revealing their symptoms, previous medical issues, and other relevant information he needs to address the patients' concerns. Typically, according to Glenn, when a new patient visits a medical doctor, he/she typically fills out a form focusing on how the doctor will get paid. In other words, physicians fall short, Gero asserts, in obtaining a "holistic" overview of the patient's medical/health profile. Glenn believes without this information, conventional medical practices shortchange the patient's road to optimal well-being.

Because naturopaths are not licensed in the state of New Jersey, they are not eligible for insurance reimbursement. In the fifteen or so states were naturopaths are licensed, they can receive insurance reimbursement. In Gero's practice, he accepts cash, checks, and credit card for payment. He does not discount his fees nor offers patients a payment plan. His website contains a page for all the services and the accompanying fees. In short, Gero provides full transparency for prospective patients. Additionally, 30 percent of his practices revenue comes from the appropriate supplements he believes patients need to achieve optimal well-being. Some patients will see Glenn for only one to three visits while others with chronic conditions will be a patient for several weeks or months.

Future of Health Care in America

How can the American people achieve optimal well-being and better health outcomes? In October 2018, Gero attended a weeklong seminar at Harvard Medical School devoted to lifestyle and mind/body medicine. The focus of the seminar session was on diet, exercise, and mind/body approaches to optimal well-being. There was no mention of pharmaceutical drugs as an appropriate protocol for patients the seminar, interestingly enough, was sponsored by the psychiatric department. Undoubtedly, psychiatrists more than any other conventional medical doctor see the relationship between the mind/body and optimal health.

One of the takeaways from the weeklong seminar is that "sitting is the new smoking." To emphasize this point, a treadmill and exercise cycle were placed at the two podiums, reinforcing the notion that motion is an integral part of increasing optimal well-being.

At the Joshlin Diabetes Center, a study of three thousand men concluded that 300 minutes per week of walking/aerobic exercises and strength training would reduce their chances of getting diabetes. For relatively healthy individuals, the current guideline is 150 minutes per week of exercise to increase well-being and health.

After more than two decades as a naturopathic doctor who began to be interested in optimal health at the tender age of twelve, Gero asserts that the American people can avert many chronic conditions if they altered their lifestyle. In other words, the nation's $3.6 trillion medical tab could decline substantially if people took more responsibility for their health care by learning what the body needs, increase their exercise, reduce stress levels, and get enough sleep. According to Glenn, we can reduce such chronic conditions as Alzheimer's, heart disease, diabetes, autoimmune issues, skin disorders, and many other debilitating illnesses that have been driving up the costs of medical care in the country.

As far as the proposals for "universal" medical insurance, Gero believes a better approach would be more competition among insurance companies, hospitals, and pharmaceutical firms. In addition, although there have been great advances in technology to detect illness before they become life-threatening incidences, Gero asserts that the proper protocol treatment is as vital to a patient's well-being and optimal health as early detection. Thus, he passionately believes that a lifestyle approach to leading a disease free life would increase substantially if people took more responsibility for their health and devote as much effort, time, and resources to their increase their well-being instead of waiting for an illness to occur and be treated with medication and surgery.

Even leading a "model" lifestyle is no guarantee of a having a chronic illness. But as Gero points out 80 percent of optimal health is controllable.

*****

How well are the American people? According to the Center for Disease Control website, six in ten adults in the United States have a chronic disease, and four in ten adults have two or more chronic diseases. These ailments include heart disease, cancer, chronic lung disease, stroke, Alzheimer's disease, diabetes, and chronic kidney disease. The medical costs of diet-related chronic diseases are substantial. The costs of obesity are $147 billion, $245 billion for type 2 diabetes, and $316 billion for heart disease. The "lifestyle" risks include tobacco use, poor nutrition, lack of physical activity, and excessive alcohol use.

In other words, we human beings are what we eat, what we drink, and inhale. And if we are sitting in front of the TV, computer screen while video gaming, and of course behind the desk at work, the lack of physical activity increases our risk for getting a chronic disease.

To put the human cost in perspective, nearly nine hundred thousand Americans die each year from heart disease or stroke, approximately one-third of all deaths recorded in America. More than 1.6 million people are diagnosed with cancer, which claims the lives of nearly six hundred thousand Americans. Rising cancer care is expected to reach approximately hundred and $75 billion by 2020.

Diabetes takes an enormous toll on the American people. Thirty million Americans have diabetes, and another eighty-four million adults are prediabetic, increasing the risk of type 2 diabetes. Diabetes could eventually lead to heart disease, kidney failure, and blindness.

The impact of obesity cannot be overstated. One of five children and one in three adults are obese, which increases the risk for diabetes, heart disease, and some cancers.

Nearly fifty-five million Americans have arthritis or about one in four adults and is one of the most common chronic conditions and common cause of chronic pain. In 2013, the costs associated with arthritis and related conditions was more than $300 billion, which included hundred $140 billion in medical costs $164 billion in lost earnings.

Alzheimer's disease affects nearly six million Americans and is the sixth leading cause of death among all adults and is the fifth leading cause for those age sixty-five or older. Current costs are estimated to be at least $200 billion, and by 2040 costs could jump *anywhere* from $379 billion to $500 billion annually.

Although life expectancy for both men and women have increased to seventy-six and eighty-one respectively, the Center for Disease Control reveals a nation of very ill adults, who have the power to reduce their chronic conditions and enjoy a better quality of life and indeed longer life.

The problems have been identified: chronic illnesses that can be reduced, if not eliminated, with appropriate lifestyle changes. So what are the dietary guidelines for the American people that supposedly will address these issues? According to the United States Department of Agriculture website, containing dietary guidelines for Americans, healthy eating should focus on the following: whole fruits, a variety of vegetables a variety of proteins, whole grains, low-fat or fat-free milk or yogurt, less sodium, saturated fat, and added sugars. More details can be found at the USDA's webpage, ChooseMyPlate.gov.

Are the USDA's dietary recommendations the best suggestions to reduce chronic illnesses in America? For decades, the American people have been told to eat a "balanced" diet that includes all food groups. However, there are naturopaths like Glenn Gero, other holistic practitioners, and medical doctors who challenge the so-called conventional diet guidelines.

One such health practitioner is Dr. Josh Axe, author of the national best-seller *Keto Diet: Your 30 Day Plan to Lose Weight, Balance Hormones, Boost Brain Health, and Reverse Disease.*

He is a doctor of chiropractic, certified doctor of natural medicine, and clinical nutritionist.

From his website, "Dr. Axe founded the natural health website *DrAxe.com*, which at over 17 million monthly visitors is considered the No. 1 natural health website in the world today. Its main topics include nutrition, natural medicine, fitness, *healthy recipes*, home DIY remedies and trending health news. His website includes a group of credentialed editors, writers and a Medical Review Board."

> The following is based on the material presented in the Keto Diet, and is not intended to diagnose any illness but only to recount Dr. Axe's journey from a concerned 13-year-old who witnessed his mother's initial cancer diagnosis to a world-renowned healthcare professional.

Josh Axe, at age thirteen, became aware of nutrition when his mother was being treated for breast cancer. One day, he saw a public service announcement (PSA) on television, which asserted that soda is bad for you. He stopped drinking soda and began to realize that food and diet might be "a better way" to deal with health issues. A decade later, he enrolled in a Florida chiropractic college and learned the foundations of nutrition and trained to become a doctor of functional medicine. He also studied how ancient remedies can improve the well-being of people.

While he was in private practice, Axe came across the ketogenic diet and soon learned that his mother was diagnosed with a tumor on her lung. He took his knowledge and revamped his mother's diet. She eliminated processed foods an added more portions of veggies, herbs, healthy protein, wholesome fat, and bone broth. Josh also suggested his mother drink vegetable juices, eat wild salmon, take cod liver oil, and consume mushrooms. Axe's mom eliminated virtually all processed carbs and added sugars from her diet.

Overtime, she had more energy, her depression lifted, and she lost twenty-two pounds. A few months later her, CT scan revealed the tumor shrunk to one-half its original size without chemotherapy or radiation. Nine months after her diagnosis, she was almost in complete remission, and thirteen years later, she's cancer-free and says she feels better now in her sixties than she did in her thirties.

Axe asserts that bolstering an individual's body's defenses with nutrition is just common sense in dealing with illnesses. He points out that the ketogenic diet will lower inflammation, correct hormonal imbalances, jump-start weight loss, transform your health so you could lead a disease-free future as much as possible.

Contrary to conventional wisdom regarding dietary guidelines, Axe recommends a high-fat diet, moderate protein foods, and very low-carb foods for optimal health. He claims the guidelines in his book can work for anybody who has tried so many diets and has failed to achieve permanent weight loss. He points out his approach is grounded in science because we should be receiving our sustenance from nature—organic plants, berries, nuts, and free-range meats. In addition, he recommends occasional fasting so the body can go into "ketosis" so it would be better able to burn fat rather than carbs for fuel.

Doctors discovered fasting in the 1920s at Johns Hopkins University and the Mayo Clinic as a way of treating patients for numerous problems such as seizure disorders and diabetes. The physicians discover that fasting can help relieve the patients of their chronic symptoms. Axe devotes considerable pages to the benefits of fasting as another "tool" to achieve optimal health.

Axe points out how fats found in avocados, coconut oil, olive oil, and salmon, to name a few of his recommendations, are actually good for your brain and heart while sugar is the "fuel" for cancer cells, which need sugar to survive. Thus, according to Josh, our bodies need vegetables, herbs, vitamins, and minerals that are the basic building blocks of health and healing. He points out that our body is 73 percent fat, 25 percent protein, and 2 percent carbs. He, therefore, asserts that the opposite of what we've been told about diet will provide us with optimal health.

In the past, diets focused on "restriction, denial, and deprivation." He points out eating well is not about counting calories but eating the right kind of foods. In short, he claims the imbalances caused by carbohydrates and sugar, especially grains and grain-fed meats, are the primary culprits in diminishing the American people's well-being.

Axe spells out the "keto plate" and what foods we should always eat and what foods we should never eat in order to have healthy productive lives. He claims we can reduce most, if not all, chronic pain and illnesses by following his ketogenic protocols, which includes high-intensity interval training.

At about the same age, Glenn Gero (twelve) and Josh Axe (thirteen) became interested in diet and better health because of personal experiences. Neither realized that a weight problem and a mother's cancer diagnosis would eventually lead both of them to careers in health care.

Today, both Glenn and Josh are using holistic approaches to help their patients achieve optimal health and well-being by focusing on the "right stuff" that we should be consuming that is consistent with our body's needs to prevent illnesses and age gracefully.

They both assert that conventional medical doctors could help their patients by integrating more nutritional recommendations in dealing with illnesses that typically are treated with prescription drugs and other medical interventions. If holistic approaches are more widely accepted in the medical profession, the current $3.3 trillion spent on medical care could be reduced substantially. And that would be a boon to families' finances, a lowering of employers' medical insurance costs, and a substantial reduction in taxpayer-financed Medicare and Medicaid expenditures on the way to a single-payer system based on personal responsibility.

Now More than Ever Personal Responsibility Is Crucial

Are we headed for public health disaster? According to Jane E, Brody, *New York Times* health-care columnist, a study published in the December 2019 issue of the *New England Journal of Medicine* (https://www.nejm.org/doi/full/10.1056/NEJMsa1909301) cited in her February 11, 2020, column ("Warnings of a Coming Public Health Disaster") forecasts that by 2030 nearly 50 percent of adult Americans will be obese and approximately one in four will be severely obese. Moreover, in half of the United States severe obesity will be greater than one in four adults, "and severe obesity will become the most common weight category among women, non-Hispanic black adults and low-income adults nationally."

The culprits for this impending "public health disaster" have been known for decades—sugar-sweetened soda, processed foods, bigger portion sizes especially in restaurants and fast-food outlets, a more sedentary lifestyle, and according to neurologist Dr. David Perlmutter, author of the *Grain Brain* and other books on health, the American people are eating too many "bad" carbohydrates, especially wheat and bad fats.

Readers can make up their own minds after reading Dr. Perlmutter's book whether their diet will create long-term medical issues such as Alzheimer's disease and other degenerative diseases. The evidence he presents is compelling and has enormous implications for future medical costs of America's aging population.

By 2030, 20 percent of the US population will be sixty-five years or older, and the cost for Medicare Part A is projected to be nearly $600 billion while the cost for Part B (physicians' bills) will be $810 billion in 2029, according to the 2020 trustees report. However, the trustees report undoubtedly does not take into account the projected deteriorating health conditions of the country's aging population nor does it factor in any acceleration in price inflation especially in the medical sector. In other words, a perfect financial storm may be forming that could overwhelm the federal budget and the ability of seniors to pay higher premiums for their Part B coverage.

The alarm bells are sounding loud and clear: an unhealthy aging population plus higher medical costs would put enormous burden on physicians and hospitals to treat the increasing number of Alzheimer's disease patients and cardiac, stroke, and cancer cases.

Both the immediate and long-term solutions are for the American people to not only lead healthier lifestyles but also to take control of the medical decisions with a single-payer system focused on the doctor-patient relationship. As we saw in previous chapters, this is easier said than done.

If the American people focus on wellness and not just treating the symptoms of illnesses, they will be able to reduce their medical costs now and in the future by hundreds and hundreds of billions of dollars per year. American living standards would increase dramatically as these funds could be used for other purposes—education, housing, business formation, leisure, and all the activities that come with improving the human experience.

We, therefore, need a cultural/financial/psychological approach for optimal health. This should be a nonpartisan issue. As former Democratic Senator Tom Harkin stated, "America's health care system is in crisis precisely because we systematically neglect wellness and prevention." And former Republican Governor and Presidential Candidate Mike Huckabee observed, "The health care system is really designed to reward you for being unhealthy. If you are a healthy person and work hard to be healthy, there are no benefits," except, of course, having optimal health, staying out of hospitals and not taking prescription drugs. As educator Maria Montessori asserted, "Personal health is related to self-control and to the worship of life in all its natural beauty—self-control bringing with it happiness, renewed youth and long life."

America's medical care system needs a reset. Government intervention for the past hundred plus years has undermined the American people's ability to achieve optimal health, quality medical care, and reasonable costs from conception to end of life. But there is a way out in the twenty-first century. The individual single-payer system where every American takes charge of his/her medical/health needs is eminently doable and imperative.

The current hybrid medical care "system" is financially unsustainable, and the American people therefore have an opportunity to take matters into their own hands but only if they are willing to embrace personal responsibility, self-control, financial independence, and increase their philanthropic activities.

The American people took care of themselves with the help of family and community before employer-based insurance, Medicare, Medicaid, and Obamacare. With all the great advancements made in medicine in the past sixty years and the knowledge we now have about nutrition and wellness, we can indeed have the best universal medical care in the world. All it will take is for the American people to have the courage to give up the false security of the current system and replace it with their own empowerment.

Chapter 6

Pandemic, Lockdowns, and the Doctor-Patient Relationship

Most COVID-19 related deaths occur among high-risk
groups who already have life-threatening conditions.
—Bill Sardi

The Bill of Rights does not say that we have in alienable rights to
freedom of speech, assembly, and religion "unless people get sick…"
—Thomas J. DiLorenzo

The economy is necessary to human life as oxygen or water.
—Michel Accad

Politics should never override the doctor/patient relationship, nor
presume to know what is better for us than our own physicians.
—Jeffrey A. Tucker

According to the Center for Disease Control website, there
were 11.3 million COVID-19 cases in the United States as
of mid-November 2020 and 247,834 deaths. At the same
time, the Johns Hopkins Coronavirus Resource Center reported 5.2
million COVID-19 cases globally and 750,000 deaths, including its

count of 166,000 deaths in the United States, slightly higher than the CDC number.

As grim as these numbers reveal, the controversies surrounding the spread of the virus, governments' reactions around the globe, including a shutdown of most of their economies in many nations, and the unorthodox treatments physicians have used to treat their patients, do we have to wait for future historians to provide us with objective assessments of the pandemic of 2020?

The voluminous number of news articles, essays, op-eds, and the widespread state and local government mandates and executive orders provides current analysts with a rich trove of material to assess the assertions made by government officials and pundits that the policies enacted to deal with the pandemic were in fact necessary and worthwhile to stop the virus and prevent millions of deaths. Or do we have to wait for the federal government to create a commission as suggested by Philip A. Wallach and Justus Myers in their Brookings essay, "The Federal Government's Component Virus Response—Public Health Timeline" (March 31, 2020) to sort out all the issues related to the spread of the coronavirus in the United States?

According to the time line provided by Wallach and Myers by mid-January 2020, the United States had very few coronavirus cases, but there was a growing concern about its spread in the Seattle area. On January 27, the White House Coronavirus Task Force was created, and a public health emergency declaration was declared on January 31. In the meantime, the WHO "sent hundreds of thousands of tests to dozens of laboratories around the world by early February." But the CDC decided to develop its own test that proved to be relatively unreliable. Needless to say, testing was not ramped up in order to determine how widespread the virus had become. By the end of February, there were only two dozen confirmed cases in the United States while China had about eighty thousand cases and Italy had nearly two thousand cases.

By the end of February, the Food and Drug Administration allowed the use of nonapproved tests, and travel bans were announced of foreign nationals who would been in Iran. In addition, an $8.6 billion bill was passed by Congress, which provided funds "promote vaccine and treatment research, emergency telehealth, and preparedness."

President Trump addressed the nation on March 11 and declared a national emergency on March 13. The federal government announced an increase in mass testing, a boost in medical supplies, and encouraged the public to take considerable measures to halt the spread of virus. Additional travel restrictions were introduced, citing the potential threats from European, British, and Irish travelers. The Defense Production Act was activated, commercial tests became common, and mass testing arrived, which revealed the spreading of the virus throughout the country. By the end of March, there were one hundred thousand confirmed cases in the United States.

The *New York Times* reported ("The True Toll of the Pandemic Climbs Past 200,000," August 14, 2020) "at least 200,000 more people have died than usual since March." With charts showing the peak in that above normal deaths in the four regions of the United States—Northeast, South, West, and Midwest—the "geography" of the pandemic shows the peak in excess deaths occurring in April and May in the Northeast and another peak for southern and western states in July. The author suggests, "Many of the recent coronavirus cases and deaths in the South and the West *may* have been driven largely by the reopening's and relaxed social distancing restrictions" (Emphasis added). The author is speculating why there was a spike in deaths attributed to the coronavirus in the south and west in the summer of 2020. Without knowing exactly the causal factor (factors), the spread of the coronavirus may in fact have been a "natural" geographical-diffusion phenomenon in the United States no different from other widespread pandemics throughout history.

Moreover, have excess deaths occurred because of increased suicides, heart attacks, and strokes? Have excess deaths occurred because individuals did not get treatment for their diabetes or cancers?

Did excess deaths occur because of drug abuse of prescription and illegal drugs? Were there excess deaths because individuals did not get diagnosed for an illness fearing to go to the doctor? In addition, have COVID-19 deaths been misclassified as some doctors have asserted? Did the use of ventilators early on in the treatment of COVID-19 patients hasten their demise?

Not all these questions will be addressed here. The key point is who should the American people trust regarding the proper response to the threat of the virus that some physicians and researchers have argued has been overstated?

Nevertheless, the "politicalization" of the coronavirus has been a reflection of the political culture that has evolved in America for the past hundred years, namely, the concentration of power and economic/medical decision-making in Washington and state capitals, which has created the political conflicts that have unfolded in our 24-7 news cycle.

In a previous pandemic (1957) Jeffrey Tucker, editorial director for the American Institute for Economic Research, reported ("Elvis Was King, Ike Was President, and 116,000 Americans Died in a Pandemic," May 4, 2020), "Like the current pandemic, there was a demographic pattern to the deaths. It hit the elderly population with heart and lung disease... The infection rate was probably even higher than the Spanish flu of 1918 [675,000 Americans died from this], but this lowered the overall case totality rate to 0.67%. A vaccine became available in late 1957 but was not widely distributed."

Based upon the data, Tucker informs us that although life expectancy (sixty-nine years) was lower in 1957 compared with today (seventy-eight years), the population was healthier with lower rates of obesity. In other words, the virus of 1957, which killed 116,000 Americans out of a total population of 172 million, "was more wicked than COVID-19 thus far." In fact, despite the high relative number of deaths that occurred in 1957 compared with the current pandemic, the economy was not shut down. Nothing was closed by order of governors, mayors, or even the president. Life went about as usual.

Ironically, the *New York Times*, which has been critical of President Trump for his handling of the coronavirus, wrote this in a September 18, 1957, editorial, "Let us all keep a cool head about Asian influenza as the statistics on the spread and the birds of the disease begin to cure. For one thing, let us be sure that the 1957 type

A influenza virus is innocuous, as early returns show, that antibiotics can indeed control the complications that may develop."

Tucker asks the most important questions regarding the pandemic of 2020 and by prefacing it with this.

> The mystery of why today vast numbers of governments around the world (but not all) have crushed economies, locked people under house arrest, wrecked business, spread despair, disregarded basic freedoms and rights will require years if not decades to sort out. Is it the news cycle that is creating mass hysteria? Political ambition and arrogance? A decline in philosophical regard for freedom as the best system for dealing with crises?

Do we have to wait for decades to sort the issues? Below, we will address some of them highlighting a theme of this book—restoring the doctor-patient relationship and how we can deal with so-called public health issues with free markets.

One of the earliest pandemics in America occurred during the American Revolution. Not only did General George Washington have to fight the British, but he also had to make sure his troops were healthy enough to fight the redcoats and not succumb to the smallpox epidemic that ravaged the nation.[19]

In 1793, when the nation's capital was still in Philadelphia, the City of Brotherly Love was gripped by yellow fever, which was not known to be the caused by mosquitoes at the time. The pandemic was responsible for killing nearly 10 percent of the city's fifty-one thousand population. Fortunately, the epidemic did not spread beyond the city limits, and precautions were taken under the leadership of Mayor Matthew Clarkson. The mayor "formed a committee of respected local citizens organized makeshift hospitals, raised

---

[19] *See "A History of Smallpox in America," Michele R. Berman, MD, https://www.kevinmd.com/blog/2011/06/history-smallpox-america.html.

money for treatment, cleaned the streets and wharfs, and looked after children suddenly orphaned when parents or guardians died from the disease."[20] In addition, Reed informs us that charity played a major role in assisting the citizens of Philadelphia during this tragedy. New Yorkers made a gift of $5,000 to the citizens of Philadelphia, a huge sum at the time, and the beginning of a widespread philanthropic effort by citizens of nearby communities to assist their fellow Americans. The short-lived epidemic (August 1 through November 9) was not the last in Philadelphia. Another yellow fever outbreak occurred in the last three years of the 1790s. The lesson from the 1793 epidemic, according to Reed, is that private charity stepped up to the plate to help the citizens of Philadelphia through their horrific experience and that the initiatives of private citizens did more to stem the outbreak than any of the minor restrictions the local government imposed to halt the yellow fever.

As far as the best-known pandemic of the past century is concerned, the so-called Spanish flu of 1918, the Center for Disease Control summarizes the events:

> The 1918 influenza pandemic was the most severe pandemic in recent history. It was caused by an H1N1 virus with genes of avian origin. *Although there is not universal consensus regarding where the virus originated,* it spread worldwide during 1918-1919. In the United States, it was first identified in military personnel in spring 1918. (Emphasis added).
>
> It is estimated that about 500 million people or one-third of the world's population became infected with this virus. The number of deaths was estimated to be at least 50 million worldwide with about 675,000 occurring in the United

---

[20] See "How the Founders Responded to an Epidemic in the Nation's Capital," Lawrence W. Reed, https://fee.org/articles/how-the-founders-responded-to-an-epidemic-in-the-nations-capital/.

States. Mortality was high in people younger than 5 years old, 20-40 years old, and 65 years and older. The high mortality in healthy people, including those in the 20-40 year age group, was a unique feature of this pandemic.

While the 1918 H1N1 virus has been synthesized and evaluated, the properties that made it so devastating are not well understood. With no vaccine to protect against influenza infection and no antibiotics to treat secondary bacterial infections that can be associated with influenza infections, control efforts worldwide were limited to non-pharmaceutical interventions such as isolation, quarantine, good personal hygiene, use of disinfectants, and limitations of public gatherings, which were applied unevenly.

However, according to retired physician Gary G. Kohls, ("The True Story of the 1918 'So-called Viral Influenza' Pandemic)[21] was not caused by influenza but by "an experimental bacterial meningitis vaccine cultured in horses by the Rockefeller Institute for Medical Research in New York…" The vaccine was injected into soldiers at Fort Riley (Kansas) who were then sent to Europe at the end of world war, where "they spread bacteria at every stop between Kansas and the frontline trenches in France." After World War I ended on November 11, 1918, returning soldiers spread the bacterial pneumonia worldwide. During the War, "the Rockefeller Institute also sent its experimental anti-meningococcal serum to England, France, Belgium, Italy and other countries, helping spread the epidemic worldwide."

Dr. Kohls points out "bacterial pneumonia attacks people in their prime. Flu attacks the young, old and immunocompromised." Thus, the CDC, based on Dr. Kohl's narrative and that of others, should revise its narrative about the so-called Spanish flu.

---

[21] https://www.lewrockwell.com/2020/07/gary-g-kohls/the-true-story-of-the-1918-so-called-viral-influenza-pandemic/.

This brings us to the current pandemic.

A Google search of COVID-19 (August 15, 2020) resulted in more than six billon hits. Good luck with that. What do we know or should know about the severity of the virus? Were lockdowns the optimal method to deal with the virus? Was the "cure" more harmful than the disease? Have we entered a "new normal"—where social distancing and wearing a mask will be commonplace?

A Swedish emergency room doctor, Sebastian Rushworth, provides a glimpse of what his country's response was to COVID-19.[22] Unlike many states in America where governors disallowed so-called nonessential businesses from opening, all businesses remained open in Sweden. In addition restaurants and cafés continued operations, schools were open, and wearing a mask in public was the exception rather than the rule.

Dr. Rushworth recounts how COVID-19 cases accelerated by mid-March and patients who typically use the emergency room virtually disappeared from his hospital; surprisingly, almost all incoming patients tested positive for COVID-19. More remarkable is the fact that Dr. Rushworth has not seen a single COVID-19 patient in over a month. When he tests patients who appear to have one of the symptoms, no one tests positive. Furthermore, he points out, the daily death rate is around five, which means that infections are virtually zero, because "people generally die around three weeks after infection." Given his experience, Dr. Rushworth concludes, "is in all practical senses over and done with in Sweden. After four months."

Moreover, according to Dr. Rushworth, six thousand Swedes have died out of a population of ten million, and those that did succumb to the virus, 70 percent were over eighty years old, many of whom would have died from other natural causes this year. The doctor concludes in a nation where one hundred thousand people die annually, COVID-19 has been "a mere blip in terms of its effect on mortality."

---

[22] "How Bad is COVID Really? (A Swedish doctor's perspective), https://sebastianrushworth.com/2020/08/04/how-bad-is-covid-really-a-swedish-doctors-perspective/.

Despite the conventional notion propagated by the media that herd immunity would not be effective in slowing down the virus, Dr. Rushworth asks, "If herd immunity hasn't developed, where are all the sick people? Why has the rate of infection dropped so precipitously?" He believes the reason there has been a substantial slowdown in infection is because T cells, the body's main defense against virus infections, have been able to protect hospital workers since the pandemic began in Sweden, which has weathered the storm relatively successfully.

Dr. Rushworth believes as many as five million Swedes have been infected with the virus out of a total population of ten million and with six thousand dead, the case mortality rate is 0.12%, "roughly the same as regular old influenza, which no-one is the least bit frightened of, and which we don't shut down our societies for."

Gilbert Berdine, MD, compares the Swedish daily mortality rate with New York, Illinois, and Texas and concludes that after reaching a peak in mid-April 2020, the rate fell consistently until August 2020, "[F]or all practical purposes, the COVID-19 epidemic is over in Sweden."

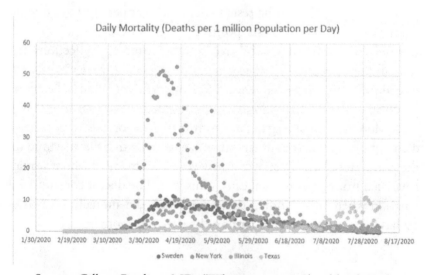

Daily Mortality (Deaths per 1 million Population per Day)

Source: Gilbert Berdine, MD, "Why Americans Should Adopt the Sweden Model on COVID-19," August 15, 2020, https://mises. org/wire/why-americans-should-adopt-sweden-model-covid-19.

In comparing the death rates of Sweden and three large US states, Dr. Berdine sums up his analysis regarding the policies for each jurisdiction.

> The data suggest that lockdowns have not prevented any deaths from covid-19. At best, lockdowns have deferred death for a short time, but they cannot possibly be continued for the long term. It seems likely that one will not have to even compare economic deprivation with loss of life, as the final death toll following authoritarian lockdowns will most likely exceed the deaths from letting people choose how to manage their own risk. After taking the unprecedented economic depression into account, history will likely judge these lockdowns to be the greatest policy error of this generation. Covid-19 is not going to be defeated; we will have to learn how to coexist with it. *The only way we can learn how best to cope with covid-19 is to let individuals manage their own risk, observe the outcomes, and learn from mistakes.* The world owes a great debt to Sweden for setting an example that the rest of us can follow. (Emphasis added)

So where did the idea of a lockdown the deal with COVID-19 originate? Jeffrey Tucker details the genesis of the lockdown idea that was based upon a simulation prepared by a fourteen-year-old high school student Laura M. Glass, daughter of Robert J. Glass, an analyst at Sandia national laboratories.[23] Glass, who is the primary author of the paper, "Targeted Social Distancing Designs for Pandemic Influenza," has no medical training and no expertise in immunology or epidemiology. Nevertheless, two government doc-

---

23 Jeffery A. Tucker, "The 2006 Origins of the Lockdown Idea," May 15, 2020, https://www.aier.org/article/the-2006-origins-of-the-lockdown-idea/.

tors, Richard Hatchett and Carter Mecher, swayed policymakers that a lockdown and social distancing would be critical in a future pandemic even though there was "intense initial opposition" to their assertion.

However, Tucker points out that Dr. D. A. Henderson, who had led the international effort to eradicate smallpox, was cited in the *New York Times* article (April 22, 2020) with a contrary view of lockdowns.

An excerpt from The *Times*'s article as reported by Tucker:

> Dr. Henderson was convinced that it made no sense to force schools to close or public gatherings to stop. Teenagers would escape their homes to hang out at the mall. School lunch programs would close, and impoverished children would not have enough to eat. Hospital staffs would have a hard time going to work if their children were at home.
>
> The measures embraced by Drs. Mecher and Hatchett would "result in significant disruption of the social functioning of communities and result in possibly serious economic problems," Dr. Henderson wrote in his own academic paper responding to their ideas.
>
> The answer, he insisted, was to tough it out: **Let the pandemic spread, treat people who get sick and work quickly to develop a vaccine to prevent it from coming back**. (Emphasis in original Tucker essay)

Henderson and three professors from Johns Hopkins, in their 2006 paper, "Disease Mitigation Measures in the Control of Pandemic Influenza," which Tucker quotes from extensively, concludes with the assertion that to combat a pandemic it is necessary for "normal social functioning of the community is least disrupted." Needless to say, given the reaction of governors, mayors, and the assertions made by

Dr. Anthony Fauci, director of the National Institute of Allergy and Infectious Diseases, the recommendations of Henderson and his colleagues were either ignored or discounted in their handling of the COVID-19 pandemic.

In short, as far back as 2006, highly respected medical professionals warned against widespread lockdowns to deal future pandemic. Proponents of lockdowns have asserted that lives were saved because the draconian measures were crucial to preventing more deaths from the coronavirus. However, the unintended consequences of essentially shutting down most of the US economy for several months caused unemployment to skyrocket, the economy to contract precipitously, and businesses throughout the country to close permanently.[24]

In addition, the unprecedented increase in federal government spending by as much as $4 trillion as of August 2020 to deal with the lockdowns while the Federal Reserve created more than $3 trillion in just a few months, causing the money supply to increase at more than a 25 percent annual rate during the first five months of the pandemic. Price inflation will probably increase in the future as the new money flows through the economy, increasing the ability to producers to raise prices as consumers have more dollars to pay higher prices.

---

[24] See one article about the devastating impact of the lockdowns, https://www.marketwatch.com/story/41-of-businesses-listed-on-yelp-have-closed-for-good-during-the-pandemic-2020-06-25 and https://www.retaildive.com/news/the-running-list-of-2020-retail-bankruptcies/571159/. Additional data for all 2020 that will be published in 2021 may reveal the worst year for retailers and small business since the Great Depression.

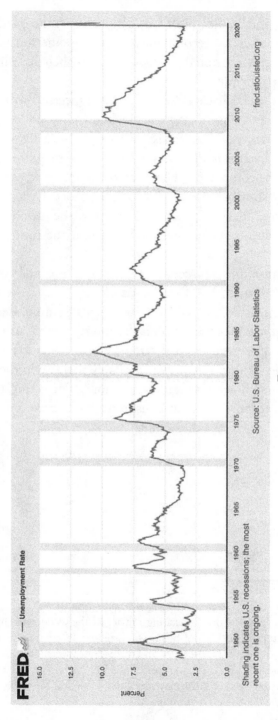

Figure 1

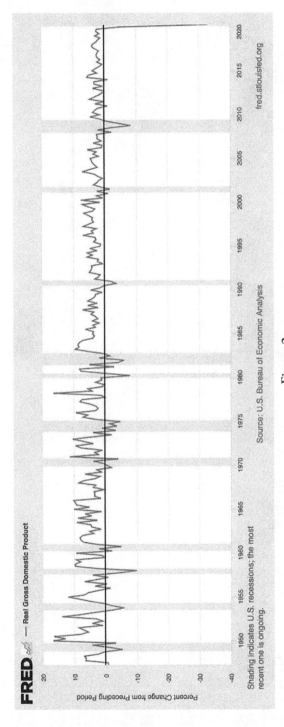

Figure 2

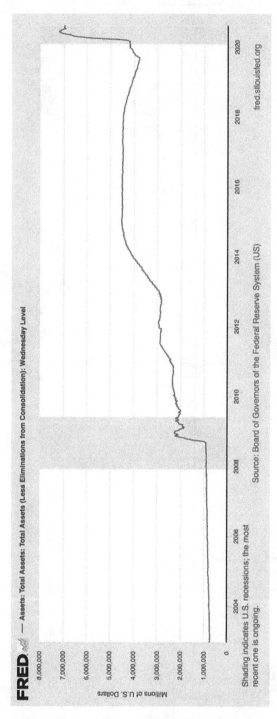

Figure 3

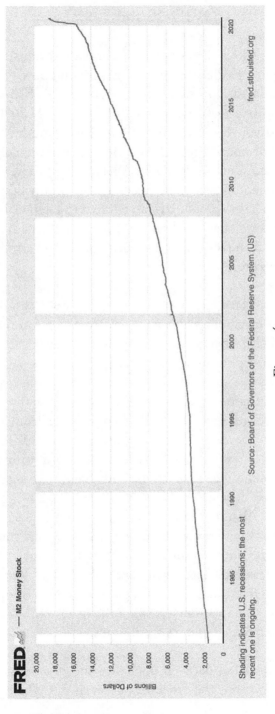

Figure 4

COVID-19 and Wellness

As the previous chapter pointed out, an individual's wellness is a full-time job. Needless to say, a substantial number of Americans have not taken the job seriously. In her *New York Times* column ("Poor Diets Role in Coronavirus Risk," April 21, 2020), Jane E. Brody cites a conversation she had with Dr. Dariush Mozaffarian, dean of the Friedman School of Nutrition Science and Policy at Tufts University. According to the dean, as relayed by Brody, less than 20 percent of American adults are metabolically healthy despite a plentiful supply of healthy food. He also referred to a national report that describes a poor diet as "the leading cause of poor health in the US," causing more than half a million deaths per year.

Thus, according to Brody,

> The characteristics of what doctors call the metabolic syndrome—excess fat around the middle, hypertension, high blood sugar, high triglycerides and a poor cholesterol profile—suppress the immune system and increase the risk of infections, pneumonia and cancers. They're all associated with low-grade, body-wide inflammation, Dr. Mozaffarian explained, "and COVID kills by causing an overwhelming inflammatory response that disables the body's ability to fight off pathogens."
>
> Alas, the metabolic well-being of many Americans is now further endangered by currently advised limits on shopping trips, an increased reliance on canned and packaged foods high in fat, sugar and salt, and emotional distress that prompts some people to turn to nutritionally questionable "comfort foods."

The connection between poor diet and disease is straightforward. It also explains the disparities between the White population and the African American, Hispanic, and people in poor communities in the both the rate of infection and rate of fatalities. Ironically, although the federal government spends about $70 billion a year for the Supplemental Nutrition Assistance Program (the former food stamps program), the program does not restrict recipients from buying unhealthy foods—those that are shown to adversely affect the immune system such as sugar, wheat, saturated fats, and other foods that the medical practitioners in the previous chapter assert undermine an individual's ability to fight off infections.

So how do low-income individuals and families who depend upon SNAP funding to purchase food change their buying habits to include more healthy foods such as fruits, vegetables, and healthy fats? There are proposals such as allowing SNAP recipients to spend a $1.30 on these healthy items for every dollar they receive, but they would be able to spend only $0.70 on the dollar for sodas and snacks.

Brody highlights several successful initiatives that help individuals and families become more nutritious conscious so they will be able to reduce their diet-related diseases. In addition Brody cites a report by Dr. Mozaffaraian and his colleagues, "Food is Medicine—The Promise and Challenges of Integrating Food and Nutrition into Healthcare," that was published in JAMA Internal Medicine as a road map for providing free nutritious meals to low-income families in order to reduce the incidence of diet-related diseases. This initiative, according to the authors, would increase school and work performance, reduce health costs, and in other words, increase productivity and wages. In other words, a so-called win-win expenditure of taxpayer dollars.

As the connection between diet and immunity is well-established, what are the other factors that individuals can control in order to ward off an infection?

According to Dr. Glenn Gero, several supplements are critical for a strong immune system that would help ward off the coronavirus and other pathogens. As always, check with your physician, naturopath, or other health-care provider as to which nutrients are best for you and what dosage is compatible with your medical condition. Everyone has a unique medical/health profile, and your responsibility is to match your needs with the following supplements Dr. Gero and others have suggested.

- Andrographis
- Astragalus
- Chaga
- Codonopsis
- Cordyceps
- Echinacea
- Elderberry
- Garlic
- Ginseng
- Goldenseal
- Licorice
- Maitake
- Melatonin
- Oregano
- Reishi
- Resveratrol
- Sage
- Selenium
- Shiitake
- Thyme
- Turkey tail
- Vitamin C
- Vitamin D
- Zinc

Longtime health writer Bill Sardi has asserted, based on his coronavirus research, that victims of the disease are woefully deficient in vitamin D and zinc, two nutrients that are essential for a strong immune system to ward off infections and how supplements can treat COVID-19 successfully.[25]

---

[25] Bill Sardi's extensive writing about COVID-19 can be found here, https://www.lewrockwell.com/author/bill-sardi/.

The Bottom Line

An overwhelming body of evidence from respected physicians, scientists, health-care practitioners, such as naturopaths, economists, and other public policy analysts, have concluded the following about the pandemic of 2020:

- Lockdowns were unnecessary to curtail the spread of the virus. The harm to the economy in terms of lost jobs, lost income, destroyed businesses, runaway federal spending, and unprecedented money printing will be felt for years to come.[26]
- Lockdowns have led to weight gain—and thus a weakened immune system—increased alcohol use, higher levels of anxiety and depression, forgoing of medical treatment, and increased suicides. The intended adverse consequences of the lockdowns when all is said and done may have led to more premature deaths than the virus. An accurate tally of premature deaths will be known in 2021 or beyond when accurate data should become available from the CDC or other agency.
- Schools should not have been closed because youngsters are relatively safe from the coronavirus. Of the nearly sixty-one million youngsters (zero to fifteen years old) in the country, those who contracted the virus, the survival rate has been 99.999926 percent. And closing schools may have both short-term and long-term adverse impacts on youngsters' health.[27]
- For the 42.9 million young people (ages fifteen to twenty-four), the CDC data as of the first week of August 2020 reveal 240 deaths from COVID-19, a mortality rate of 0.56 per 100,000, slightly higher than the 0.45 per 100,000

---

[26] A Google search of the health consequences of the lockdown returned more than fifty million hits.

[27] See Allysia Finley, "Lockdowns and School Shutdowns May Make Youngster Sicker," *Wall Street Journal,* August 12, 2020.

annually from influenza and pneumonia. Colleges and universities could have stayed open with the proper protocols in place to limit the spread of the virus.

- The 6.5 million Americans aged eighty-five and older had a mortality rate of 700.5 per 100,000 as of August 1, 2020, or 80 percent of the COVID-19 deaths. Together with the two other age groups, fifty-five to sixty-four and sixty-five to eighty-four, 92 percent of COVID-19 deaths occurred in these three age groups.

- Hydroxychloroquine has been used successfully by physicians in treating COVID-19 patients throughout the world but has been discounted—and heavily criticized—by Dr. Fauci, the medical establishment and virtually all the journalists and talking heads in the establishment media as a viable treatment in this pandemic.[28]

- The open letter cited below concludes with the following: **"It is essential that you tell the truth to the American public regarding the safety and efficacy of the hydroxychloroquine/HCQ cocktail.** *The government must protect and facilitate the sacred and revered physician-patient relationship by permitting physicians to treat their patients.* Governmental obfuscation and obstruction are as lethal as cytokine storm" (Emphasis in original for the first sentence and second emphasis added by the author).

- Retired cardiac surgeon Donald Miller outlines the case against wearing a mask and how vitamin deficiencies have contributed to the death rate from COVID-19.[29]

---

[28] See the open letter by three physicians to Dr. Fauci, https://www.thedesertreview.com/opinion/columnists/open-letter-to-dr-anthony-fauci-regarding-the-use-of-hydroxychloroquine-for-treating-covid-19/article_31d37842-dd8f-11ea-80b5-bf80983bc072.html. Also see, Mary Beth Pfeiffer's essay, https://www.nj.com/opinion/2020/05/dont-doubt-hydroxychloroquine-because-trump-is-taking-it-it-likely-works.html.

[29] See https://www.lewrockwell.com/2020/08/donald-w-miller-jr-md/covid-19-and-the-1918-20-spanish-flu-a-progressive-century-apart/.

Looking Ahead

Will a vaccine to combat COVID-19, which is currently under development by several pharmaceutical companies, allow the US economy to return to "normal"? Under Operation Warp Speed,[30] the Trump's administration program to rush a vaccine to the American people, the hope is that an effective vaccine will stop the virus in its track and allow life as we knew it to resume.

However, Bill Sardi asserts that a mass vaccination is not about saving lives. A summary of his Q&A essay format should give the public, physicians, and policymakers pause regarding a coronavirus vaccine.[31]

> Humanity is racing to coerce, propagandize and eventually mandate vaccination of the entire world's population, skipping safeguards and pre-buying vaccines before they are proven safe or effective. Over 100 vaccines are reported to be under development and some have entered clinical trials. Yale University is exploring advertising messages that are the most convincing. Their initial survey found 67% of participants would accept a COVID-19 vaccine.
>
> A problem is the public is likely to never hear of the side effects and deaths caused by vaccination because it is so easy to blame fatalities on the virus itself. Given the information presented in this report, there is a high possibility that a vaccination catastrophe awaits as governments push to vaccinate for obvious political and financial reasons.

---

30 See https://www.hhs.gov/about/news/2020/06/16/fact-sheet-explaining-operation-warp-speed.html.

31 See https://www.lewrockwell.com/2020/08/no_author/its-not-about-saving-lives/.

There are suspected motives to reduce the number of older Medicare recipients now that its trust fund is being depleted by fewer contributions due to COVID-19-related unemployment. Part of Medicare funding now comes out of the general fund of the United States as the Trust Fund can no longer bear the full burden of this system. The per capita Medicare spending for 85-year-olds is 2.5 times greater than for 66-year-olds. While the chance for dying among children age 0-19 from COVID-19 coronavirus is 0.003%, it is 7.836% among 80-year-olds! The fact that nearly 7 in 10 Americans would accept a largely untested vaccine suggests a naïve population that is direly in need of un-biased education.

A vaccine consent/refusal form is now available at Covid19Consent.com that educates Americans about the risks and benefits of COVID-19 vaccines.

Even if a vaccine became available in the future, it may be ineffective for a substantial portion of the population, those that have body mass index of thirty or more. As Sarah Varney discusses in her essay, "America's Obesity Epidemic Threatens Effectiveness of Any COVID Vaccine,"[32] obese individuals have suppressed immune systems "putting obese people at greater risk of infection from pathogens such as influenza and the novel coronavirus. In the case of influenza, obesity has emerged as a factor making it more difficult to vaccinate adults against infection. The question is whether that will hold true for COVID-19."

Nevertheless, Varney cites a study conducted by UNC-Chapel Hill scientists that "showed for the first time that vaccinated obese adults were twice as likely as adults of a healthy weight to develop

---

[32] https://khn.org/news/americas-obesity-epidemic-threatens-effectiveness-of-any-covid-vaccine/.

influenza or flu-like illness." Although the obese subjects did produce sufficient antibodies to ward off the influence, "they still responded poorly." According to Chad Petit, an influenza virologist at the University of Alabama, obesity may interfere with T cells, the white blood cells that are needed for a strong immune response. He believes a vaccine can be developed to better protect obese individuals from the coronavirus.

Even if no viable vaccine(s) is developed, is the world doomed to reoccurring pandemics for the foreseeable future? Not if we continue to rely on so-called experts in and outside government who assert a top-down approach to public health is necessary to stem any pandemic.

As we have seen in 2020, the coronavirus pandemic has been an up close and personal case study of government overreach, where governors and mayors have issued mandates based upon CDC guidelines to "bend the curve" of the number of infected with the virus and reduce the number of deaths to zero.

Optimal wellness, personal responsibility, private property, and the free market would do more for stopping any future potential pandemic.

As we have seen in the previous chapter and in this chapter, a substantial number of Americans have weakened immune systems, especially the elderly who are most vulnerable to any virus. Thus, maintaining optimal well-being is a major factor in fighting off any coronavirus now and in the future.

If an individual does contract a coronavirus, he/she should isolate himself to protect their neighbors and coworkers. No government mandate is necessary. Employers have the absolute right to deny access to the workplace of anyone who shows symptoms of influenza. Employers also would have the right to make remote work mandatory. There was no need for governors or mayors to compel office, mall, or small businesses closures while allowing so-called essential businesses to remain open. If we believe in the rule of law and equality, all businesses should have been allowed to stay open. In the next pandemic, all businesses must be treated equally.

The main takeaway from the lessons of the 2020 pandemic is that a free market and equality under the law would have improved the public health outcomes in dealing with the coronavirus. This is not rhetoric but the conclusions of well-respected scientists, physicians, and policymakers in the United States and from around the world.

If we believe that we should "follow the science" to formulate public policy, then current policymakers need to bring into the discussion the individuals who challenge the status quo regarding treating the coronavirus with hydroxychloroquine, wearing masks in public, and shutting down most of the economy to stop the spread of COVID-19.

The past hundred-year march toward greater collectivism in America so far has reached the pinnacle with the reaction to the coronavirus. During this period, collectivism has failed throughout the world—in the former Soviet Union, communist China, and in the remaining socialist hellholes like Cuba and North Korea. And let's not forget the horror of the collectivist agenda of National Socialism that Hitler imposed on the German people and Europe.

If there is a main lesson of the 2020 pandemic is that the people cannot put their faith, trust in political figures for their well-being. As well-intentioned as governors and mayors have been, it is the people's responsibility to make medical decisions in consultation with their physicians.

Yes, we can have high-quality, low-cost universal medical care without the government involved in making medical decisions or paying it with, of course, taxpayers' money.

The $64,000 question is, Are the American people ready to take charge of their medical care? Or do they want to continue relying on the middlemen—their employers and insurance companies, Medicare and Medicaid—for their medical care?

The status quo means seeking a job with the "right" medical insurance, staying on a job they may dislike because the employer provides generous medical benefits, continuing to navigate the insurance maze, and occasionally having to battle with an insurance company for benefits. No more under a single-payer system where every individual and family is in charge of their medical coverage.

Old habits, so to speak, are hard to break, but if the American people want to have better health outcomes at a fraction of the cost they are currently paying for high-priced insurance, the material in this book provides a road map for a healthier America where everyone receives high-quality medical care from conception to end of life.

Chapter 7

Toward the Individual Single-Payer Medical Care System

If the goal of health-care reform is to provide comprehensive,
universal healthcare in a cost-effective way, the only
honest approach is a single-payer approach.
—Bernie Sanders

But the very people who are marketing the idea of "universal
coverage" want us "covered" so they can control medical care.
—Jane M. Orient, MD

If war is too important to be left to generals, then medical care—erroneously called health care—is too important to be left to politicians and bureaucrats. In addition, there is absolutely no reason for medical insurance to be an employee benefit. After all, individuals and families purchase all kinds of insurance—automobile, homeowners, life, etc.—in the private marketplace, where prices are reasonable and coverage is virtually universal. And there is no need for "insurance" to pay for virtually all medical costs for an individual and families. In short, the American people are "overinsured." We do not need insurance coverage to see a doctor for a sore throat, other non-life-threatening illness, or a medical test. Insurance is only necessary to pay for a major medical illness that otherwise would be out of the reach for the average American family.

So how did we get here? Why are individuals so dependent on medical coverage through their employer? And why is the government paying for more than half of all medical costs through Medicare, Medicaid, and subsidies through Obamacare? The simple answer is government intervention and ideology. World War II created the conditions with wage-price controls, which led employers to provide medical coverage as an employee benefit to circumvent the government's restriction on raising wages during labor shortages of the global conflict. And the logic of the welfare state ideology promoted the notion that health care is a "right," and thus, every individual is entitled to medical care just because they are Americans, and therefore, it is the duty of the government to help pay for, or provide, medical coverage especially for low- and middle-income individuals and families.

As we have seen, the proponents of government universal medical care have been successful in incrementally increasing the federal government's role in medical care for the past three quarters of a century. The great leap forward came in 1965 with the creation of both Medicare and Medicaid and in 2010 with the passage of Obamacare. And today, the support for a so-called public option, where individuals and families would have the ability to "buy in" to Medicare, is astonishingly high. It is another incremental step toward a government universal medical care system.

Make no mistake about it, the endgame of government intervention in medical care would be a complete takeover of medicine in America.

As Dr. Jane Orient, executive director of the Association of American Physicians and Surgeons (AAPS), succinctly describes the dilemma we are in regarding the calls for government universal medical care—the single-payer system advocated by Sen. Bernie Sanders and others,

> We got ourselves into our current dilemma
> by trying to repeal the laws of economics, and

now we are trying to cope with it by repealing the laws of ethics. We must not ignore the fact that all of this rhetoric about the "universal right to healthcare" has very serious implications. Being covered by health insurance by no means guarantees you medical care. On the contrary, the more medicine is socialized, the less medical care you can count on receiving. If you have the right to all the health care that society determines you are entitled to but cannot afford to provide that means you have no right to live.[33]

There is, however, a way to have "universal medical coverage" without the need for employer-based insurance, Medicare, Medicaid, Obamacare, or any other government involvement in the doctor-patient relationship. All the "pieces" are currently in place to make the doctor-patient relationship the center of the nation's medical care system. For individuals and families, that means using their income to make the basic choices for routine medical care with a physician in private practice or with a clinic in pharmacies and big-box stores.

Funding a health savings account instead of employers paying for expensive "health insurance" would provide the financial resources for individuals and families to pay for routine doctor visits, prescription drugs, and medical tests. This would be an enormous step toward "patient empowerment." Catastrophic medical coverage would be the only insurance individuals and families would require, avoiding the financial burden of a major illness.

In a free market, prices gently drift lower as the supply of goods and services increases. The same would be true for all medical expenses, especially pharmaceutical prices. And without the need to file insurance forms, doctors would not have to hire a mini army of administrative staffers to send claims to insurance companies, Medicare, and Medicaid. The administrative costs in a free market

---

[33] Janet Orient, "Healing America: The Free Market Instead of Government Health Care," Notes from FEE, September 2006, p. 3.

health-care system would plummet, spreading the benefits to both doctors and patients. Physicians would see their overhead costs drop precipitously, and those savings should be reflected in lower fees to patients.

As far as poor and low-income families are concerned, they, too, would benefit from lower medical prices and the creation of throughout the country of more nonprofit centers modeled after Volunteers in Medicine. The American people are the most generous individuals on the planet. We could make the case that philanthropy is in the American people's DNA. Charitable contributions, which would be deducted dollar for dollar on an individual's federal income tax return—a tax reform that would create a huge incentive for philanthropic donations—would lower the tax burden and thus provide the financial resources for individuals and families to fund thousands of new nonprofit medical centers in low-income areas. Nonprofitization would increase substantially throughout the country and create the most widespread social safety network in American history.

Given the current ideology and political culture in America, the notion of free market medical system seems like a pipe dream. But at one time, more government intervention in medical care was considered inconceivable. Nevertheless, since the time greater government intervention in medicine was first proposed, every generation has had articulate advocates for socialized medicine. Thus, we have been headed down the government single-payer system road for several generations and even so-called fiscal conservatives in and out of government have been warming up to the idea of greater government involvement in medical care.

In the final analysis, government intervention, that is, mandates, regulations, price controls, and other forms of coercion distort economic activity and tend to raise prices for consumers. As economist Thomas J. DiLorenzo observed, "Government never, ever, reduces the cost of doing anything." In addition, Lenin, the first leader of the Soviet Union, "called medicine the keystone in the arch of socialism."[34]

Do the American people want to be dependent on the government for their medical care? Do they want to depend on politicians and faceless bureaucrats to determine what treatment they can have or cannot have? Do physicians want to be bound to politicians and faceless bureaucrats in the federal government and insurance companies to tell them how to practice medicine? These are the fundamental questions the American people need to answer—and soon. The march toward socialized medicine continues, and if so, the American people should be careful—very careful—what they wish for.

As Benjamin Franklin famously remarked, "They who can give up essential liberty to obtain a little temporary safety deserve neither liberty nor safety."

A free market, single-payer (the individual) medical care system would give the American people both liberty and security. But more importantly, it will give them high-quality medical care and lower prices.

---

[34] Orient, ibid, p. 2.

Index

About the Author

Murray Sabrin arrived in America from West Germany with his parents and older brother on August 6, 1949. His parents were the only members of their respective families to survive the Holocaust.

In 1959, at age twelve, Sabrin became a US citizen and graduated from the Bronx High School of Science in 1964. He has a BA in history, geography, and social studies education from Hunter College, an MA in social studies education from Lehman College, and a PhD in economic geography from Rutgers University.

Dr. Sabrin joined the faculty of Ramapo College of New Jersey in 1985 and retired on July 1, 2020, where he was professor of finance in the Anisfield School of Business. He taught Financial History of the United States among other courses. In 2007, he and his wife, Florence, made a $250,000 gift to Ramapo College to establish the Sabrin Center for Free Enterprise in the Anisfield School of Business (www.ramapo.edu/sabrincenter). In 2020, the Sabrins donated $50,000 to create the Sabrin Center resource room in the new Peter P. Mercer Learning Commons to house Murray's collection of economic, finance, history, and philosophy books and monographs.

Sabrin is the author of *Tax Free 2000: The Rebirth of American Liberty*, a blueprint on how to create a tax-free America in the twenty-first century, and *Why the Federal Reserve Sucks: It Causes, Inflation, Recessions, Bubbles and Enriches the One Percent*, which is available on Amazon.

In 1997, Sabrin was the New Jersey Libertarian Party's nominee for governor and made political history when he raised sufficient funds to participate in the state's matching funds program, which required him to participate in three debates with the two major party candidates. He also has sought the Republican nomination for the US Senate in the Garden State.

CPSIA information can be obtained
at www.ICGtesting.com
Printed in the USA
FSHW010025130921
84723FS